Partners for Innovation In
Teaching and Learning

Partners for Innovation In Teaching and Learning

✦

A Shared Responsibility

Sharon L. Silverman and Martha E. Casazza

iUniverse, Inc.
New York Lincoln Shanghai

Partners for Innovation In Teaching and Learning
A Shared Responsibility

iUniverse books may be ordered through booksellers or by contacting:

iUniverse
2021 Pine Lake Road, Suite 100
Lincoln, NE 68512
www.iuniverse.com
1-800-Authors (1-800-288-4677)

ISBN-13: 978-0-595-35067-4 (pbk)
ISBN-13: 978-0-595-79773-8 (ebk)
ISBN-10: 0-595-35067-4 (pbk)
ISBN-10: 0-595-79773-3 (ebk)

Printed in the United States of America

Contents

Preface

We have had the privilege of working with faculty across the College of Professional Studies at New Jersey City University for several years. We first met this very dedicated group of professionals in the Fall of 2001 when we were invited by Dean Bloomberg to make a presentation based on our book, *Learning and Development*. Following this initial session, the faculty shared their teaching strategies and invited us into their classrooms. They were all extremely eager to discuss innovative ideas and ways to improve their teaching. We had many brainstorming sessions where everyone shared both their successes and challenges. These were followed by individual consulting sessions where critical feedback was given, and new strategies were formulated collaboratively between the consultant and the faculty member.

From the early days of face to face sharing and classroom visitations, there evolved a community of professionals who trusted one another enough to continue discussions online through a Web Board. Everyone was issued an ID and a password, and we all "talked" both synchronously and asynchronously. After a few years of sharing among the group, known formally as the *Partners for Innovation in Teaching and Learning*, we all decided to hold a daylong symposium. On October 10, 2003, the group came together to tell their teaching stories based on reflections related to best practice in the classroom. The symposium was a great success and attracted the attention of faculty outside the group who were excited to hear these very real stories of innovations in teaching. It was videotaped and subsequently edited and formatted by the consultants. This tape is available through the Dean's office and serves as an excellent resource for anyone interested in improving their teaching.

Our long term collaboration with this faculty would not have occurred without the support of the Dean, Dr. Sandra Bloomberg, and her assistant, Melanie McDonald. They made our regular visits possible and also ensured that all logistical arrangements were efficiently organized. The Dean's office also set up a Web Board early in our collaboration so that the partners could have ongoing conversations between our visits. It is evident that the administration of the College of Professional Studies is committed to supporting and encouraging the professional development of its faculty.

The faculty we have worked with in the College of Professional Studies represents a hardworking, caring group of individuals. They are very much committed to their students and to improving the quality of their educational experiences. Each one has been willing to critically reflect on practice and to take the risks necessary to try something new. We have sincerely enjoyed our work with this faculty and have learned a great deal from them.

Sharon L. Silverman
Martha E. Casazza
Consultants

Introduction

In this monograph, you will find five articles written by faculty members at New Jersey City University (NJCU). The articles emerged from participation in a teaching and learning series called *Partners for Innovation in Teaching and Learning.* From 2001 to 2005, a group of teachers from the College of Professional Studies at NJCU met periodically to address issues of teaching and learning in their classrooms. The group was facilitated by Martha Casazza and Sharon Silverman, educational consultants in higher education.

As a result of participating in *Partners for Innovation in Teaching and Learning,* the participants were introduced to a framework called *TRPP* (Theory, Research, Practice, Principles) that provides a way to apply theories and research to challenges we meet with our students. *TRPP* was developed by Casazza and Silverman (1996) and Silverman and Casazza (2000) to help cross the divide between theory and practice.

The underlying assumption of *TRPP* is that no one theory adequately explains all behaviors in every situation. An eclectic approach that includes facets of different theories is most useful in developing instructional strategies for increasingly diverse groups of students. The *TRPP* framework exists to integrate different theoretical perspectives and research findings to better understand what educators do, why they do it, and how it ultimately leads to learning outcomes. The opening article in this monograph describes the *TRPP* framework in detail and elements of the *TRPP* framework are evident in each of the subsequent articles. Six participants from the original group share how they have applied new ideas in their teaching practice. Each article represents a blend of theory, research, and practical strategies.

Margarita Martinez—Sheehan shares an experience she had teaching a course for the first time. In her article, *"Shared Responsibility for Learning"*, she describes how she developed partnerships with her students to develop the course syllabus and learner-centered activities. She tells how she made connections with the special interests of her students, created a climate of active engagement with shared responsibility, and even arranged the physical setting of her classroom to promote her goals. Margarita shares her frustrations and challenges as she achieves a learner-centered environment and provides inspiration for those willing to try a new approach.

Michael Krantz and Bill Soo Hoo have described, through a review of the literature and their own classroom experience, a model that helps us shift from a teacher-centered approach in education to one that calls attention to student outcomes and assessment. Their article, *An Alternative Problem-Based Collaborative Learning Model and Student Experiences*, provides a new approach to student-centered learning that reflects a combination of successful elements from problem-based learning, learning communities and collaborative learning. Their model can be implemented in a single class as opposed to some of the more costly alternatives that are dependent on a series of paired courses for student cohorts.

In her article, *Movement Training: an Integration of Body, Mind and Emotions*, Jan Schlegel introduces us to a teaching method where emotions, thoughts, and physical talent are the basis of learning. The importance of emotions in learning has been increasingly recognized, but we are not always confident to address this in our teaching. While Jan discusses physical development, the principles in her article can be applied to other subjects as well. In her article, student quotes are used extensively to convey the effect of this approach. How can movement and emotions be a part of learning in a variety of disciplines? This article offers the opportunity to reflect on this important question.

In her article, *"The Question is the Answer"*, Rosalyn Young underscores the importance of the desire and ability to ask questions as a precondition for active learning. Using Chaffee's categories of questions, she guides her students through the process of developing questions based on assigned readings. Students participate in the development of a question rubric and are more enthusiastic as a result of developing it themselves. Throughout the article, Rosalyn tells how she engages her students actively through the use of questioning skills. Her approach is applicable to all disciplines and provides a framework for using questions as a vehicle for more active participation in the learning process.

Finally, James Brown in his article, *"Lessons Learned: Engaging Students by Creating Community in Online Courses"*, guides us into the concept of building community in the online classroom. Using group dynamics theory, Jim adapts principles to online learning. Just as in the regular classroom, creating community with online learners results in better learning, retention, and overall satisfaction. Jim takes us on a journey with his experience in online course development and includes specific strategies to make this learning format active and engaging. With the increase in online learning throughout higher education, this article is especially timely and pertinent.

As you read through this monograph, we expect you will be stimulated with new ideas to use in your teaching practice. These authors have "been there and done it" and through their challenges and successes, they have much to offer those who are open to change.

Contributors

Margarita Martinez-Sheehan, MS.Ed is an Assistant Professor in the Fitness, Exercise & Sports Department at New Jersey City University. She is currently a doctoral candidate in Educational Leadership at Rowan University in Glassboro, NJ. She received her graduate degree in Physical Education from Queens College, NYC and her BA in Dance and Physical Education from Herbert H. Lehman College, NYC.

Michael S. Krantz, Ph.D. is an Assistant Professor of Criminal Justice/Security at New Jersey City University. He has authored and facilitated hundreds of programs in Law Enforcement, Security, Human Capital, Leadership and Assessment in the public, private and education sectors. Dr. Krantz was a certified consultant for the Anti-Defamation League and The National Conference for Community and Justice since the early 1990s. He worked extensively with the Attorney General's Office of Bias Crimes and Community Relations developing curricula and conducting in-service training statewide. Mike earned his BA from Rutgers University, and his MA and Ph.D. from Seton Hall University.

Tsung Y. (Bill) Soo Hoo, an Assistant Professor and Security Program Coordinator at New Jersey City University's Criminal Justice/Security Department, is currently completing his Ph.D. in Higher Education Administration and Supervision at Seton Hall University. He retired from the FBI after 31 plus years of service as a Special Agent, and has been in "Who's Who Among America's Teachers" in his first two of three years of teaching at NJCU.

Jan Schlegel, M.A. is Professor and Chairperson, Fitness, Exercise & Sports Department in the College of Professional Studies at New Jersey City University. She received her M.A. in Art Education from New Jersey City University and her M.F.A. in Dance from NYU School of the Arts. She will be a guest speaker at the International Congress of Cognitive Psychotherapy in Goteborg, Sweden June 13-17th 2005 as part of a panel that explores physical applications in conjunction with psychotherapy.

Rosalyn Young, J.D. is an Associate Professor of Business at New Jersey City University. As a member of the Critical Thinking Rubric team, she developed and drafted the campus-wide Critical Thinking Rubric. She also served as Chair of the Student Assessment Forum for the School of Professional Studies and is a member of the Political Science Pre-Law Advisement Board. She received her law degree from Brooklyn Law School and a certificate of advanced graduate study in business from Pace University.

Dr. James W. Brown, the Dean of Health Sciences and Human Performance at Ocean County College, Toms River, New Jersey, has received numerous awards for innovative practices in health care and public health, and for online instruction. Dr. Brown pioneered the first online courses at the College of Professional Studies at New Jersey City University and has been a developer/co-designer on over 30 online courses. He received the 2003 Lloyd M. Felmly Award for outstanding contribution in the media to the cause of public health in New Jersey for his pioneering work in online courses in public health and health care. He is the principle investigator on a Robert Wood Johnson Foundation New Jersey Health Initiatives (NJHI) Workforce Agenda Grant to develop an online education model to address shortages of RNs in the hospital setting. Dr. Brown received a B.A. from Rutgers College and an M.S. and Ph.D. in Microbiology from the Waksman Institute of Microbiology at Rutgers University and a Masters of Science in Health Sciences from Jersey City State College now New Jersey City University (NJCU). Dr. Brown continues to teach his online courses as an Adjunct Professor for NJCU.

TRPP: Bridging the Great Divide

Sharon L. Silverman

"I'm a teacher. I don't have time for theory and research, and anyway why bother? I work with students. I need to spend time on lessons not research studies. Let the theorists and researchers do their work. I'll focus on my students."

Developmental educators put their students first. They should. Their students need caring, committed teachers who can provide the best learning environments. The challenges are great. Teachers must be patient, supportive, encouraging, inventive, and indefatigable. Who has time to bother with theory and research?

Typically, teachers teach, researchers test hypotheses, theorists construct theories. The work of theorists and researchers may seem remote to those in the classroom. There is often a great divide. Valuable information from research is often not applied in real educational settings. We need to bridge the gap, to make connections between what we know about student learning and how we educate. We need a framework for effective practice.

TRPP (Theory, Research, Practice, Principles) was developed by Casazza and Silverman (1996, 2000) to help cross the divide between theory and practice. *TRPP* is a framework to connect theory and research findings and apply them to practice. The underlying assumption of *TRPP* is that no one theory adequately explains all behaviors in every situation. An eclectic approach that includes facets of different theories is most useful in developing instructional strategies for increasingly diverse groups of students. The *TRPP* framework exists to integrate different theoretical perspectives and research findings to better understand what educators do, why they do it, and how it ultimately leads to learning outcomes.

Using the Framework

There are four components in *TRPP*: Theory, Research, Principles, and Practice. The four components function together within a process of critical reflection with the ultimate goal of maximizing student potential. The framework is circular promoting the notion that its use does not begin nor end at a certain point. Instead, use of the framework is an ongoing process so the educator may begin with any of the four components and move through them in any order depending on a particular situation or inclination. Throughout the process, critical reflection is employed in the review of information and its application to student learning.

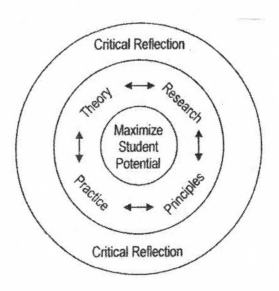

Here is how *TRPP* might be used in your practice. Think of a challenging situation you are facing. What is troubling you about it? How have you tried to address the situation?

After identifying the challenge, begin with one of the four *TRPP* components. As mentioned earlier, you may begin at any point in the framework. You could start by looking for theories that address the issue, or with a principle you've tried, or with something you've observed in your practice. For purposes of this example, let's start with research—R—to see what studies may have revealed about this challenge. Then move and find theories that connect to the research, construct a principle to guide you in meeting this challenge, and then finally, apply the principle to your practice. Here's an example to illustrate the process.

Challenge

Students aren't taking responsibility for their own learning. They expect the teacher to provide all the necessary information and don't actively engage in the learning process. When asked to discuss ideas in class, there is little response.

Research

What does research say about the challenge of student responsibility? There is a great deal of information on this topic. When addressing student responsibility, the topic of motivation seems pertinent. If students aren't taking responsibility, maybe it's because they aren't motivated. Let's look at some of the research concerning student motivation to learn and see how it could address the challenge.

One of the key research findings in motivation concerns goals. Are students learning with performance or mastery goals? Performance goals are those that involve comparison with others and competition. For example, a teacher who gives test results comparing students to each other is using performance goals. The emphasis is on the group average, and individual students are judged according to how their performance met, surpassed, or fell below the mean. With performance goals, competition is the key. With a performance goal orientation, successful students strive to outperform their peers. Teachers encourage competition believing that is motivates students to perform well.

Mastery goals are oriented toward self-improvement without comparison to others. The notion of competition with others is absent. Instead a mastery goal orientation focuses on learning that provides opportunities to set goals for personal achievement not connected to the performance of others. An individual goal is chosen and becomes the focus of the learning activities. For example, in a foreign language class, a student learning with mastery goals might identify a number of new vocabulary words to use in a writing assignment and strive toward this goal. In contrast, with emphasis on a performance goal, the student would try to use more new vocabulary words than other students in the class. The students using the most new words performs "best" while others using less are compared to the best student and graded accordingly.

Research in performance and mastery goals has yielded some interesting findings. When students are in environments that emphasize performance goals, they tend to focus on memorization without emphasis on problem solving or critical thinking. They are more inclined to be directed toward short-cuts and quick payoffs. Students, who are learning within a mastery goal orientation, are more likely to use comprehension monitoring, which includes elaborating, as well as organizing strategies for relating new material to past experience. (Maehr and Anderman, 1993). Research on goals and learning has produced consistent results showing that an orientation toward mastery goals leads to more engagement in the learning process and a higher incidence of metacognitive strategies (Maehr and Pintrich, 1995).

What do these findings have to do with student responsibility? With mastery goals leading to more engagement in learning, we would expect to see higher levels of student responsibility in a mastery learning environment.

Lock and Latham's research (1990) focused on factors related to the environment that influence goal choice and commitment. When individuals have higher norms for performance, they tend to set higher personal goals for themselves. The researchers also found that peer group support or lack of support affects individual commitment. One implication for classroom instruction is the idea that cooperative learning groups have the potential to influence a reluctant student to be more engaged in a learning activity. In addition, this research leads us to recognize the importance of helping learners identify norms that are relatively high in order to encourage the setting of higher personal goals. Research in this area helps us to understand how student responsibility is connected to goal setting and peer interaction.

A major review of cooperative learning studies in higher education was conducted by Johnson, Johnson, and Smith (1991). Evidence from these studies shows that cooperative learning has many positive effects. These include productivity, more positive relations among students, increased social support, and improved self-esteem. Student responsibility is likely to be increased when cooperative learning environments are established.

Haworth and Conrad (1997) propose a model of engagement that is also relevant to student responsibility. In their model, interaction among students with each other and with teachers and administrators is a key to success. This interaction among all participants takes place in an environment characterized by critical dialogue, integrative learning, and risk taking. So, in addition to mastery goals and peer interaction, student responsibility can be connected to wider engagement outside the classroom with others in the institution as well as to levels of risk taking. We can infer from this model that students who become more comfortable with taking risks would be more engaged in learning and likely to be more responsible.

A variety of other research findings help us address the challenge of student responsibility. When students are actively engaged in the learning process, they learn more than being passive recipients of instruction (Cross, 1987). Students report that they enjoy classes in which the instructor attempts to relate material beyond the classroom (Eison and Pollio, 1989). Lindner and Harris (1992) suggest that the ability to self-regulate in the learning process is a "basic skill underlying successful learning". In their research, Linder and Harris found a significant relationship between GPA and the amount of self-regulation used. They also found that self-regulated learning seems to increase with age and experience. From this we might infer, that older more experienced students are more likely to be responsible learners through the use of self-regulation strategies. Younger, less experienced learners are likely to need more guidance and direction in the pursuit of responsibility.

This is only a sampling of research as it relates to student responsibility. Through the findings of research in the areas of motivation, engagement, and self-regulation we can gain insights to help address the challenge.

Theory

One of the theories that relates to the challenge of student responsibility is Vygotsky's Theory of Cognitive Development. According to Vysotsky (1965), learning is a constructivist activity that emphasizes social interaction and adaptability. In contrast to the traditional view where knowledge is considered foundational and is held by experts who impart information to others, the constructivist view is a "socially constructed sociolinguistic entity and learning is inherently an interdependent sociolinguistic process (Bruffee, 1993, p. 3).

One of the key components of Vygotsky's work is the idea of a zone of proximal development. An individual's zone of proximal development is the area between latent ability and realized potential. He proposes that in order for successful learning to occur, a person must receive guided instruction leading one across the zone. This guidance comes from an external mediator who gradually releases the responsibility of learning to the learner. As the responsibility is released, a process called "scaffolding" occurs whereby the teacher provides learners the opportunity to extend their current skills and knowledge. Progress is made through steps that become increasingly more challenging within the learner's zone of proximal development. In addition, a strategy of "reciprocal teaching" takes place involving teachers and students in a discourse around content and not simply activities around questions and answers. The importance of social interaction is inherent throughout emphasizing the need for significant interchange with the environment.

A much earlier theorist, Kurt Lewin, also emphasized environmental interaction in the learning process. Lewin's theory (1936) puts forth the idea that behavior is a result of person-environment interaction. Structuring the learning environment to provide for connections to real-life experiences promotes person-environment interactions that produce meaningful behaviors. Paying attention to the individuals and the nature of the environment in which they are learning is essential. If we want to achieve student responsibility, according to Lewin, we will need to provide environments to encourage it and to focus on how individuals interact to achieve their goals.

Vygotsky and Lewin are two theorists whose ideas are relevant to the student responsibility challenge. There are others as well including Perry (1970) who contributed his stages of cognitive development from dualistic through commitment, McClusky (1970) whose concept of environmental influence on learning is that of power versus load, and Moos (1986,1979) whose theory of social climate pertains to individual learner comfort. Using TRPP, the educator would explore these theorists and others to gather a foundation connecting to Research, Principles, and Practice when addressing this challenge.

Principles

Starting with Research and moving to Theory, the next step is the development of principles for addressing the challenge. Research has shown that mastery goals lead to more involvement than performance goals. In addition, we learn from research that active engagement in learning leads to commitment while providing opportunities for individual choice in developing learning goals leads to more engaged and responsible learning outcomes.

The theoretical work of Vygotsky, Lewin, and others provides the foundation for addressing the challenge of student responsibility from a constructivist and social interaction point of view. With this background, we begin to develop principles to guide our practice.

Here is one principle emerging from Vygotsky's work: *Gradually increase the responsibility to the learners during the duration of the course.* Using Vyogtsky's notion of a zone of proximal development, this principle underscores the importance of not expecting fully developed learner responsibility from the beginning. Instead, the teacher must provide graduated steps leading to the development of learner responsibility. Using this principle in a three-session class, the following sequence would take place.

Session 1.   **Provide a preview of information prior to an explanation.**

When introducing a topic, ask students what they might already know about it. Encourage them to share their experiences and to connect them to the topic. Support guessing and risk taking. Share your own experiences related to the topic. Provide a visual overview incorporating student responses.

Session 2.   **Pause during explanations and have students write questions about the content.**

When explaining a concept, pause frequently. Ask students to write what they are thinking about it. How has the information surprised them? What don't they understand? What would they like to understand more fully? Collect their responses. Use them in further explanations and expansions on the topic. Engaging students in this way increases their attention, leads to motivated learning, and helps promote learner responsibility.

Session 3.   **Have students summarize content on an index card at the end of the explanation.**

Once a topic has been explored, create opportunities for synthesis and summarization. This can be done in small steps limiting responses to the size on an index card. Students use their own words to create summaries and are moving away from rote memorization. They may also include their own thoughts and opinions. Collect the cards or have the students share them with each other for comparison.

Building up to summarization activities in this way helps to insure student success and learner responsibility.

Here are some other principles that might emerge from using *TRPP* to address the challenge of responsibility.

> *Focus on mastery goals to promote learner motivation and responsibility.*
> *Provide opportunities for individual choice and control in learning activities*
> *Use social interaction in the classroom.*

Using (T) Theory and (R) Research to produce (P) Principles leads to (P) Practice where strategies and approaches such as the three-session example above are utilized. Practice examples for the additional principles suggested may come to mind as you construct your own learning environments.

Critical Reflection

TRPP includes the four components above but critical reflection is essential to the process. As you proceed through the four components of the framework, you engage in critical reflection—a process of closely examining and analyzing information, searching for meaning, discovering inconsistencies, and questioning the basis for one approach over another. Some approaches may work best with younger students, others with adults. Depending on the populations sampled, some research findings may be more useful than others. For example, William Perry conducted his research with male students in higher education, and his findings may not be totally useful with female students. Instead, the work of Belenky (1986) who studied female ways of knowing would be more appropriate. Critical reflection helps us make decisions that are best for the learners we teach.

The ultimate goal of using the *TRPP* Framework is to maximize student potential. We want to facilitate learning as much as possible for each individual. With the great amount of diversity among today's learners, it is increasingly important to engage in critical reflection to produce a successful learning experience for as many students as possible. Putting students first requires using theory and research in our practice. *TRPP* is a tool to reach this goal.

Reprinted with permission from The Learning Assistance Review.

References

Bruffee, K.A. (1993). Collaborative learning: Higher education, interdependence, and the authority of knowledge. Baltimore: Johns Hopkins University Press, 3.

Casazza, M.E., & Silverman, S.L. (1996) Learning assistance and developmental education. San Francisco: Jossey-Bass.

Cross, K.P. (1987). Teaching for learning. AAHE Bulletin, 39, 3-7.

Eison, J., & Pollio, H. (1989). LOGO!!: Bibliographic and statistical update. Mimeographed. Cape Girardeau, MO: Southeast Missouri State University, Center for Teaching and Learning.

Johnson, D.W., Johnson, R.T., & smith, K.A. (1991) Cooperative learning: Increasing college faculty instructional productivity. Washington DC: The George Washington University, School of Education and Human Development. (ASHE-ERIC Higher Education Report, No. 4).

Haworth, J.G., & Conrad, C.F. (1997). Emblems of quality in higher education: Developing and sustaining high-quality programs. Boston: Allyn & Bacon.

Lewin, K. (1936). Principles of topological psychology. (F. Heider & G.M. Heider, Trans.) New York: McGraw-Hill.

Linder, R.W. & Harris, B.R. (1992). Teaching self-regulated learning strategies. Washington,DC: U.S. Department of Education, Educational Resources Information Center. (ERIC Document Reproduction Service No. 362, 182).

Lock, E.A., & Latham, G.P. (1990). A theory of goal setting and task performance. Englewood Cliffs, NJ: Prentice Hall.

Maehr, M.L., & Anderman, E.M. (1993). Reinventing schools for early adolescents. Elementary School Journal, 93, 593-610.

Maehr, M.L., & Pintrich, P.R. (Eds.) (1995). Advances in motivation and achievement (Vol.9, pp.159-181). Greenwich, CT: JAI Press.

McClusky, H.Y. (1970). An approach to a differential psychology of the adult potential. In S.M. Grabowski (Ed.), Adult learning and instruction. Syracuse, NY: ERIC Clearinghouse on Adult Education.

Moos, R.H. (1979). Evaluating educational environments. San Francisco: Jossey-Bass.

Moos, R.H. (1986). The human context: Environmental determinants of behavior. Malabar, GL: Krieger.

Perry, W.G., Jr. (1970). Forms of intellectual and ethical development in the college years. Troy, MO: Holt, Rinehart and Winston.

Silverman, S.L. & Casazza, M.E. (2000) Learning and development: making connections to enhance teaching. San Francisco: Jossey-Bass.

Vygotsky, L.S. (1965). Thought and language. New York: Wiley.

Shared Responsibility for Learning

Margarita Martinez-Sheehan

This article recounts the journey with my students as we shared responsibility for learning in a sports law class. From the moment I was assigned to teach the Legal Aspects of Sports course I faced several challenges, the first being that the previous instructors left no course material for me to model or guide my process. The only guide was the catalog's single sentence description of the course. Prior to this course, I had always entered the class on the first day with a prepared syllabus. My syllabus contained clearly stated course expectations regarding assignments. This time I only had raw notes. Committed to my professional development and research in the scholarship of teaching, I took the opportunity to apply my developing skills. Having little to work from I decided to utilize my students in sharing the responsibility for developing the syllabus for the course. "Happily, most students appreciate it when we admit that we too are voyagers" (Turchi, 2004, p.5).

Starting with the course description, I had the students share their interpretation of what Legal Aspects meant to them. It was from this ground work that themes emerged and the framework for our course came about. Grauerholz, (2001), Hiemstra & Sisco (1990) & Grunert (1997) view the syllabus as a possible learning contract interactively agreed upon between students and teacher. By starting the course with the students influencing the design of the curriculum, I developed a level of trust with my students deeper than any relationship I have had with previous classes. This is the story of the learning process we took.

Reflecting on my early education and learning difficulties with traditional teaching methods, I was interested in using teaching methods that inspire and motivate students to self-direct their own learning (Goleman, 2000). My research in Educational Leadership theories influenced how I viewed myself in the role as a teacher and laid the foundation for my teaching philosophy.

Leadership Styles

Owens (2001) divides educational leadership into two categories, traditional and progressive. Traditional leadership encompasses any form of leadership where power is vested upon an individual by outside forces and the subordinates must yield to the leader. In education, the teacher is ordained as the bearer of knowledge to be imparted on the student and therefore the leader. The student as the learner listens and passively receives information and instruction from the teacher (Bonwell, & Eison, 1991, Schutz, 2004).

Progressive leadership encompasses all the theories where leadership arises from the individuals within the group to share in the leadership process. Learning becomes a shared responsibility and partnership between students and teacher. There is more freedom for student creativity and interaction with each other. The teacher moves from the traditional role of directing all activity and imparting information to students, to a role of facilitating learning and engaging students in the responsibility for their own learning. Through these humanistic approaches to leadership, the individuals of the group are empowered.

The classroom becomes a dynamic laboratory for experimentation and discovery. This type of environment has potential for a powerful impact on both students and teacher alike (Berson, Engelkemeyer, Oliaro, Potter, Terenzini & Walker-Johnson, 1998, Johnson, 1992). Shared responsibility requires the teacher to experiment with untraditional or unfamiliar teaching approaches. Progressive education focuses on student-centered learning as opposed to traditional education that promotes teacher directed activities. A goal in student-centered learning is a collaborative relationship between teacher and students. There is no hierarchy is this type of learning. All members of the group share in the decision making. Taking active roles the students become participants in the learning process (Bonwell & Eison, 1991) by responsibly directing their own learning. Wu & Short's (1996) research implies empowerment is emphasized through involvement in decision making. My students became members of a team that collectively defined the course objectives; choose the instructional methods to learn by, class projects to demonstrate their learning, and assessment techniques to determine their level of success (Astin & Astin, 2000).

Goals

Through my research on leadership theories, I learned about Robert Greenleaf's Servant Leadership style. The servant leadership style emphasizes service to others. Using a holistic approach, a servant leader promotes a sense of community through collaboration and the sharing of decision making. For the servant leader, service is the means through which consciousness comes forth as a willingness to grow spiritually (Spears, 2002). Greenleaf's servant leadership philosophy resonated with my developing philosophy of mind-body-spirit. It became my mission to assist students in helping themselves learn. Teaching has become a means in my inner growth and continuing my research and exploration into current teaching theories and applications; I have not only impacted my students but have helped myself grow spiritually. Parker Palmer (1998) wrote that the educator must develop the inner self to reach the hearts of students. Balancing intellectual, physical, and spiritual self is critical when creating a supportive environment for personal growth (Bolman & Deal, 2001). My goal was to create a supportive learning environment for the students and myself where in depth dialogue could develop thus enable opportunities for personal growth. Ultimately, my goal was to enhance student learning using a servant leadership teaching style.

Learning Community

As part of my professional development and search for a supportive environment for growth, I joined a learning community, a team of twelve New Jersey City University faculty members, called "Partners for Innovation". "Partners for Innovation" a Carnegie supported program worked to support faculty inquiry, stimulate classroom innovation and strengthen student learning (Gale, 2004). Our team explored the use of innovative learning/teaching techniques under the mentoring of two visiting educational consultants, Dr. Martha Casazza and Dr. Sharon Silverman. Using a Web CT format, group meetings and individual mentoring with the educational consultants, the team was able to reflect on teaching and learning methods.

"Partners for Innovation" had a powerful impact on my teaching style. The positive and supportive learning environment created in this team fostered my confidence as an educator to provide initiatives on student learning. Educators seeking ways to enhance student learning need supportive learning communities that provide mentors, resources, and safe environments to explore and discover themselves. "Without positive attitudes and perceptions, students have little chance of learning proficiently, if at all (Marzano, 1992 p. 18). Through self discovery teachers feel they have the capacity to bring about student learning and empowerment in their students as well (Wu, & Short, 1996).

Teaching Philosophy

My leadership style stems from a holistic philosophy that is concerned with student empowerment, emphasizing the development of the full potential of each individual. A holistic teaching philosophy encompasses the promotion of personal growth, self-actualization, development of values, treating students as individuals, valuing self-esteem, fostering personal and social development, and promoting self-responsibility in others (Wuest, & Bucher, 2003, p. 31). Grauerholz (2001), experienced in using a holistic teaching approach, views holistic teaching as a conscious means to achieve deep and lasting learning in students. Using active learning engages students in personal exploration, helping students to make connections with course material to their own lives (Grauerholz, 2001).

Using a facilitative role, I established myself as part of the group and not the dominating force in the class. Facilitative leadership involves a process that creates favorable conditions allowing followers, in this case students, to enhance their individual and collective performance (Berson, et. al., 1998, Horn, 2001). Guiding the student's process and putting a framework to their ideas became my role. I became a facilitator of learning rather than giver of information. Our task as educators is to help students understand that they can take more responsibility for their own learning (McKeachie, 1999). Guiding students involves active listening, authentic responses, and revising or abandoning familiar teaching techniques. "This process requires us to allow ourselves to be led" (Turchi, 2004, p5).

Themes

Incorporating leadership theories and applications into my classes allowed me to share with my students, ownership in their learning process. Two themes evolved from this process: sharing responsibility for learning and using a student-centered approach to teaching. My partnership with the students started with our collaboration on designing the syllabus and continued throughout our entire process.

Learning became a group interaction rather than a teacher to student interaction. Students choose interactive learning environments that are inclusive over traditional settings in classrooms that are looking for the "correct responses" and do not promote sharing of ideas. When students are welcomed, supported and listened to, they feel good about themselves. Supporting opportunities for students to experience self-efficacy is paramount for students to empower themselves (Cox, 2002). Empowered individuals gain the ability to transfer those feelings of success to new learning situations. Group learning promotes deeper learning and forms supportive relationships among group members (McGlynn, 2004).

Not only did learning become more meaningful for the students but the experience became more satisfying to me. When I began to release my authority over to the students, I became a more powerful influence on their learning process. As a member of this group I could experience the students' process and as their facilitator, I had the privilege of observing the group process unfold. This dual role provided me with immense satisfaction. "Students expect instructors to give them something useful and interesting…they trust us to understand what they need to know and how they will come to know it "(Turchi, 2004, p. 5). Given permission, students quickly took the reigns in directing their own learning yet trusted me to still guide them.

As the course progressed, students self-initiated inquisitive analysis of sport law. Their enthusiasm for learning inspired my creativity to find sources, research tools, and strategies to assist their process. During group activities the students became active in critical discussion, decision making, problem solving and were self-motivated to do their weekly assignments. Bonwell & Eison (1991) found that students that are actively engaged are involved in higher-order thinking tasks such as analysis, synthesis, and evaluation.

As sport enthusiasts, the students were well versed in sport history and professional team statistics so reading and discussing sport law cases involving their favorite teams and players became a fun and engaging activity for students. Intrigued by their discoveries, students took every opportunity to engage their discussions and inquiries outside the classroom, during their breaks, and sometimes spilling over into my office. Students were making new connections with things that interested them. "As students talk about what they know and what they are learning, their knowledge and understanding deepen" (Huba & Freed, 2002, p. 24). "I began to love my journey, and students came along for the ride" (Turchi, 2004, p. 5).

Student Responsibility

To hold students responsible we must engage students to take ownership of their learning. In order to promote ownership I structured tasks so that each member was required to participate in order to accomplish the goal, thus creating individual accountability and group interdependence. As educators we must model for the students. In the beginning I had to first provide examples of different roles group members might play and then allowed the students to elect which roles to model. For example, one member might be responsible for organizing the information and another might help decide how to present it (Marzano, 1992). Ultimately, the goal is for students to become independent learners who have developed the ability to continue to learn throughout their lives (Marzano, 1992).

Linking students' interests

If educators expect students to succeed at classrooms tasks, they must somehow link those tasks to student goals (Becker & Glascoff, 2005, Hiemstra & Sisco, 1990, McKeachie, 1999, Palmer, 1998, Paul & Elder, 2002). "Some powerful ways of doing this include allowing students to structure tasks around their interests, allowing students to control specific aspects of tasks, and tapping students' natural curiosity" (Marzano, 1992, p25). The value of learning is enhanced by knowing the students' motives and interests and linking tasks to their interests. Relate content whenever possible to issues and problems and practical situations in the lives of your students (Becker& Glascoff, 2005, Paul & Elder, 2002). They need practice thinking through problems to develop critical thinking skills and apply concepts to real life experiences. Design classroom structure to include opportunities for students to apply the fundamentals of the subject. It is only when students apply what they are learning to actual situations or problems that they come to see the value in what they are learning (Paul, & Elder, 2002).

Knowing that many of the students were actively participating on athletic teams during this time allowed me to create learning experiences that would allow utilization of their team building skills in classroom experiences. I incorporated sport terminology into classroom activities (Becker & Glascoff, 2005, Cox, 2002, Coakley, 2004) such as; captain, team cohesion, leadership, coach, judge, rules, competition, and playing in the "zone". Students passionate about their professional teams and players were able to make connections to legal issues (Davis, Mathewson, & Shropshire, 1999).

Student Goals

Through small group discussions, students expressed their desire to learn specific categories of sport law using an affordable, easy to understand text that could be covered in one semester. The problem I found in searching for a sport law textbook was that most sport law texts fell into these two categories, sports law books written for law professors teaching in law school or text focused on risk management for non lawyers (Miller, 2004). Learning legal fundamentals related to the sport management discipline should also be the goal of a sport law text (Cotton, Wolohan, & Wilde, 2001). I consulted an attorney to assist in my search for a text that would meet the student's needs. To the satisfaction of the students I found "Sports Law: In a Nutshell" by Champion (2000). To supplement the legal definitions I recommended using "Dictionary of Legal Terms: A Simplified Guide to the Language of Law" 3rd ed." by Gifis (1998).

Needing a basic knowledge to build from, we began the course by learning legal terminology, principles, and basics of legal concepts. Once we had a basic knowledge of law we began examining case studies. Students find it easier to remember legal principles when applying them to real situations as in case studies, by-passing rote learning used in traditional teaching (Becker & Glascoff, 2005). Students benefit by learning how to reason, discriminate and judge legal principles and by examining their application in real situations. Students practiced collaborative learning in small group sessions, gained understanding of legal principles, confidence by practicing their skills, and respect for their peers.

Framework

Using a basic sport law book as their guide, a pocket size legal dictionary and access to sports law organizations, students began classifying, researching, and explaining cases and legal principles. Through lively discussions students were able to apply legal principles to predict the outcomes of unresolved legal cases. I facilitated questions that served as catalysts for more in-depth class discussions. Asking students to explain legal principles as they applied to the case at hand provided a way to reinforce the learning process and knowledge in the subject.

I had students participate in team building group activities which included the supplemental reading and team presentations of case studies. The students had to summarize the main issues of the case identifying the plaintiff and defendant, the court deciding the case, facts of the case, and the courts decision. This task allowed the students to demonstrate their ability to organize and synthesize material as well as practice public speaking skills. After each presentation the class provided feedback to the team on their presentation. Thus the students learned to constructively assess each other strengths and weaknesses and provide feedback to further improve future performance.

Final Project

This active-learning process engaged students so much that they wanted to act out a legal scenario as their final project. A debate format was decided on as the venue for the final project. I researched debate formats and models and presented information to students. The students chose the topic: ("Should College Athletes Be Paid?"), negotiated captains, pro/con teams, and then began gathering research to support their prospective pro/con positions. To my pleasant surprise one student volunteered to become a facilitator for the debate. With confidence, the students expressed their desire to lead the entire debate. Once groups separated into two competitive teams my role became less of an active participant and more of a resource assistant. This undertaking required me to provide a camera, break out rooms, handouts, newsprint pads, and recruiting two impartial judges. My responsibilities became that of a coach on the sidelines supporting my team as they ran the plays. Our roles as facilitator must be flexible to meet the needs of the students as their roles evolve. The students were now leading me!

The final class sessions were devoted to the teams meeting, sharing research, forming strategies, and assigning responsibilities and final roles in debate. I utilized the time to guide the student facilitator in his role of leading the debate. Through collaborative consulting, the student facilitator and I drafted the final format and rules to the debate. When the subject of penalties arose, the student facilitator suggested using yellow and red cards, like those used in soccer, to identify and define the severity of the penalty. This is an example of a student demonstrating his linking of prior knowledge of soccer into the debate, a classroom experience.

Assessment

In teacher directed classes, students view learning as a process of figuring out what the teacher expects from the students, then fulfilling those expectations. In the debate those expectations don't exist. Students view learning as a means to achieve their own goal, winning the debate. Students form teams and help each other learn. As part of the team effort individuals take on specific roles based on their strengths and ability to demonstrate learning. By this point the students were now teaching each other so I extended that responsibility to include assessing each others contributions to the team thereby encouraging individual responsibility. The debates were filmed so the students could view themselves and assess their own performance and develop strategies for self improvement. The final student assessment included a self assessment, a peer assessment, an assessment of our methods, and an assessment of my facilitative role.

Climate

Creating a trusting environment for students to feel uninhibited is critical. My experience and sense of mutual respect developed in previous courses was instrumental in building that trust. Building true teamwork is the result of building trust and respect among a group (Jaworsky, 1996). Taking risks is part of my journey as a servant leader. "A willingness to take risks, especially the risk of inviting open dialogue, though I never know where it is going to take us" (Palmer,

1998, p. 69) required me to trust the process. Palmer (1998) reflects my thoughts in creating a classroom climate that is both hospitable and charged. "A space where students are challenged as well as welcomed" (Palmer, 1998, p. 79) creates an inviting learning environment for students' insights and stories. Classroom environments must be open for students to explore new discoveries, yet have a climate of safety to deal with the risks taken when covering difficult issues.

Traditional furniture arrangement separates the instructor from the students and creates a learning environment where the instructor is the bearer of knowledge (Hiemstra & Sisco, 1990, Schutz, 2004). A formal learning environment also distinguishes the instructor as the evaluator, thus leading the students to try to figure out what the instructor wants or expects (Hiemstra & Sisco, 1990). Arranging the seating in a circle and having the instructor as part of the circle removes the formality (Hiemstra & Sisco, 1990, McKeachie, 1999, Marzano, 1992, Schutz, 2004), and allows the individuals to look at each other as equals thus promoting collaborative conversations. Cooperative group activities create a safe learning environment that allows students to share feelings, synthesize materials and make connections to their intellect (Marzano, 1992). Learners have the ability to take responsibility for their own learning. This involves making choices regarding the learning approach, establishing evaluative criteria, and seeking appropriate resources (Hiemstra & Sisco, 1990).

Recommendations

My recommendations to aid in development of a facilitative leadership style include the following.

1. Rearrange the furniture in the classrooms to an informal setting and sit among the students. This will help to remove the stigma of the teacher as the evaluator. (Hiemstra, & Sisco, 1990)

2. Encourage students to share their stories and experiences so that they know those experiences are important. Learning is not about getting the answers but the experience in looking for the answers. As traditional educators, we were taught that we were supposed to supply the answers, but students learn more from problems that do not have convenient answers. Trust in the process of students finding their own answers.

3. During class, faculty should stay focused on the course objectives. Faculty are there to guide the students learning, not to have students perform appointed tasks.

4. Student centered learning takes time to develop. Plan for a task to take a certain amount of time but be flexible and know when the objective of the task has been reached. Having clearly defined objectives as well as clearly defined methods of assessing those objectives will aid the students and faculty in knowing when those objectives have been reached.

5. Engage students in the assessment process, this leads to student empowerment.

6. Periodically videotape your lesson and view the video with a critical eye to reflect on your current practices. Our behaviors should reflect how we see ourselves as leaders (Bensimon, 1989).

7. Learning episodes seem most meaningful when grounded in the experience of the learner.

Conclusion

This story in sharing responsibility for learning was evidence of students and teacher coming together to form shared values and commonality. "In the end, it wasn't about me; it was about what all of us did by working together. Leadership is a relationship." (Kouzes & Posner, 2002, p. 78). Using my shared leadership approach to teaching, I applied my teaching philosophy in this uncharted territory of teaching a new and unfamiliar course. I now view the syllabus not only as a contract but as a work in progress. After meeting with the students we make adjustments or refinements to the syllabus in order to meet the individual needs of the students.

My debate format was presented as a model of innovative techniques at the "Sharing Responsibility for Teaching and Learning" symposium in the Fall of 2003, New Jersey City University. My presentation was made through reflection, story telling, power point presentation and use of video clips showing the students engaged during the debate. As an educator, I modeled for other educators my ability to help others help themselves grow (Kouzes, & Posner, 2002). As a servant leader, I too will continue to reflect on my role that I play in the lives of service to others. I will continue to discover and grow as I too help others grow in the process.

References

Astin, A.W. & Astin, H.S. (2000, May). *Leadership reconsidered: Engaging higher education in social change.* Battle Creek, MI: W.K. Kellogg Foundation.

Becker, C., & Glascoff, M.A. (2005). Linking lessons and learning: A technique to improve student preparation and engagement with subject materials. *American Journal of Health Education, 36*(1), 51-53

Bensimon, E. M. (1989). The meaning of "Good Presidential Leadership": A frame analysis. *The Review of Higher Education, 12*(2), 107-123.

Berson, J., Engelkemeyer, S., Oliaro, P.M., Potter, D.L., Terenzini, P.T., & Walker-Johnson, G.M. (1998, June 2). Powerful partnerships: A shared responsibility for learning. Retrieved October 22, 2004, from http://www.aahe.org/teaching/tsk_frce.htm

Bolman, L.G., Deal, T.E. (2001). *Leading with soul: An uncommon journey of spirit.* San Francisco: Jossey-Bass.

Bonwell, C. C., & Eison, J. A., (1991, September) Active learning: Creating excitement in the classroom. Retrieved February 17, 2005, from http://www.carniefoundation.org/CASTL/higered/scholars_program.htm

Champion, W. T. Jr. (2000). *Sports law: In a nutshell* (2nd ed.) St. Paul, MI: West Group.

Coakley, J. (2004). *Sports in society: Issues & controversies* (8th ed.) New York: McGraw Hill Higher Education.

Cotton, D. J., Wolohan, J.T., Wilde, T. J. (2001). *Law for recreation and sport managers* (2nd ed.) Dubuque, IO: Kendall/Hunt Publishing Company.

Cox, R.H., (2002). *Sport psychology: Concepts and applications* (5th ed.) New York: McGraw Hill Higher Education.

Davis, T. Mathewson, A.D., Shropshire, K. L. (1999). *Sports and the law: A modern anthology.* Durham, NC: Carolina Academic Press.

Gale, R., (2004). The "magic" of learning from each other. *Hispanic Outlook in Higher Education, 15*(5), 31.

Grauerholz, E. (2001). Teaching holistically to achieve deep learning. *College Teaching, 49(2), 44-50.*

Gifis, S. H., (1998) *Dictionary of legal terms: A simplified guide to the language of law* (3rd ed.) Hauppauge, NY: Barron's Educational Series, Inc.

Goleman, D. (2002). Primal leadership: Realizing the power of emotional intelligence. Boston, Ma: Harvard Business School Press.

Grunert, J (1997). *The course syllabus: A learning-centered approach.* Bolton, MA: Anker Publishing Company, Inc.

Hiemstra, R., & Sisco, B. (1990). *Individualizing instruction: Making learning personal, empowering, and successful.* San Francisco: Jossey-Bass.

Horn, R. A. (2001). Promoting social justice and caring in school and communities: The unrealized potential of the cohort model. *Journal of School Leadership, 11,* 313-333.

Huba, M. E. & Freed, J. E. (2000). *Learner-centered assessment on college campuses: Shifting the focus from teaching to learning.* Needham Heights, MA: Allyn and Bacon.

Jaworski, J. (1996). *Synchronicity: The inner path of leadership.* San Francisco: Berrett-Koehler Publishers, Inc.

Johnson, D. W. & others (1992, February) Cooperative learning: Increasing college faculty instructional productivity. Retrieved February 19, 2005, from http://www.carniefoundation.org/CASTL/higered/scholars_program.htm

Kouzes, J. M., & Posner, B. Z. (2002). *Leadership the Challenge* (3rd ed.) San Francisco: Jossey-Bass.

Marzano, R. J. (1992). *A different kind of classroom: teaching with dimensions of learning.* Alexandria, VA: Association for Supervision and Curriculum.

McGlynn, A.P., (2004). Empowering students: Learning styles, teaching strategies. *Hispanic Outlook in Higher Education,* 15(5), 22-24.

McKeachie, W. J. (1999*). Teaching tips: Strategies, research, and theories for college and university teachers.* Boston: Houghton Mifflin Company.

Miller, L. (2004). Sports law [Review of the book *Sports Law*] *Journal of Legal Aspects of Sport,* 14(1) 113-115.

Owens, R. G. (2001). *Organizational behavior in education: Instructional leadership and school reform.* (7th ed.). Boston, MA: Allan and Bacon.

Palmer, P. J. (1998). *The courage to teach.* San Francisco: Jossey-Bass.

Paul, R. & Elder L. (2002). *A miniature guide for those who teach on: How to improve student learning: 30 practical ideas.* Dillon Beach, CA: The Foundation for Critical Thinking.

Spears, L. (1994). Servant leadership: Quest for caring leadership. *Inner Quest,* #2. Retrieved November 1, 2002, from http://www.greenleaf. org/leadership/read-about-it/articles/Quest-for-Caring-Leadership.html

Schutz, A. (2004). Rethinking domination and resistance: Challenging postmodernism. *Educational Researcher,* 33(1), 15-23.

Turchi, P. (2004, December 3). An itinerary for guiding students. *The Chronicle of Higher Education,* B5.

Wu, V. & Short, P. M. (1996, March). The relationship of empowerment to teacher job commitment and job satisfaction. *Journal of Instructional Psychology,* 23, 85-9.

Wuest, D. A., & Bucher, C. A. (1999). *Foundations of physical education and sport.* (14th ed.) Boston, MA: McGraw Hill.

An Alternative Problem-based Collaborative Learning Model and Student Experiences

Michael S. Krantz, Ph.D.
Professor Tsung Y "Bill" Soo Hoo

Introduction

Educators and policy makers continue to struggle with stakeholder demands for institutions of higher education to meet the diverse needs of students and for more effective means of delivering these services. Calls for colleges and universities to demonstrate accountability and increase efficiency are likely to become more insistent (Banta, Black, and Lambert, 1999). With the growth of higher education, come the inevitable demand for accountability and the need for a measure of success for policies and procedures in meeting desired outcomes (Trow, 1973). A number of studies have indicated that traditional education methods fall short of employer and student expectations. Graduates are not prepared with the competencies necessary to undertake professional responsibilities. Concerns have been raised that the ways students are taught do not lead them to acquire needed knowledge or skills, nor do they help them apply this knowledge and skills appropriately (Roeber, 1995). The challenges of competing in a global market where technological changes require innovative business solutions has generated the need for high-performing workers with a high level of critical thinking skills. This environment has necessitated the development of a workforce capable of going beyond the traditional task performance where guidelines are easily spelled-out. The market expects workers at all levels to solve problems, create ways to improve the methods they use and engage effectively with their co-workers (Bailey 1997; Packer 1998).

Fifty years ago teaching dominated the process of education. Educational programs were teacher-centered where faculty decided what all students had to do in order to fulfill the requirements of the institution. Increasingly, movements to consider student outcomes, student assessment and the refocusing of the institutional mission toward student learning are growing. This paradigm shift has moved from the "instructional" paradigm to the "learning" paradigm (Barr & Tagg, 1995.) Consequently, faculty have been encouraged to view teaching as "helping the students learn", rather than "covering the content" (Svinicki, 1990).

One of the most identified means of relating the goals of higher education to students' learning is in the study of teacher-student relationships and the various learning frameworks impacting student experiences and development. There has been significant research on the various models focused on teacher-student relationships, collaborative learning, problem-based learning and learning communities. The research clearly indicates a positive correlation between effective programs based on these pedagogical frameworks and positive student experiences. Whether at the undergraduate, graduate, or doctoral level, the perceived quality of relations among students, faculty, and administrators can make independent, positive contributions to student effort and desired outcomes (Kuh, Vesper, & Krehbiel, 1994).

In 1987, Arthur W. Chickering and Zelda F. Gamson published, "Seven Principles for Good Practice in Undergraduate Education", an essay that was the outgrowth of a series of special conferences investigating ways to improve undergraduate education. The seven basic principles they formulated reflected a multitude of research that identified that the most effective undergraduate learning was active, cooperative, and demanding. These principles included a strong emphasis on faculty-student contact and related processes, identifying that positive contact between faculty and students led to increased student responsibility for their own education and greater learning (Chickering & Gamson, 1991). According to Chickering and Gamson, good practice in undergraduate education encourages the following:

1. Contact between students and faculty

2. Reciprocity and cooperation among students

3. Using active learning techniques

4. Giving prompt feedback

5. An emphasis on time on task

6. Communicating high expectations

7. Respecting diverse talents and ways of learning (Chickering and Gamson, 1987).

Although these guidelines work for many different categories of students (e.g., race, economic status, gender, and level of preparation), the challenge is to develop effective methods of delivery and assessment that support these guidelines in a cost—effective and comprehensive manner. The most important determinants of student change in college have nothing to do with what is being taught, and much to do with the nature, extent, and quality of interactions between students and faculty; students and peers; and the seven principles identified by Chickering and Gamson.

There needs to be a greater focus on developing and implementing systematic methodologies an instructor can apply in a single college class setting that will impact students' perceptions and experience in order to help them learn. The literature shows that over 600 studies have been conducted during the past 90 years comparing the effectiveness of cooperative, competitive, and individualistic efforts. Johnson and others (1992) state that cooperative learning research demonstrates higher achievement, more positive relationships among students, and healthier psychological adjustment than do competitive or individualistic experiences. These effects, however, do not automatically appear when students are placed in groups; for cooperative learning to occur, the professor must carefully structure learning groups (1992). Successful groups depend on a variety of factors including group size, establishment of a group culture fostering equal group effort, recognition of individual contributions to the group's work, and the cohesiveness, responsibility, and commitment among group members (Abrami et al. 1995). It would seem that attempting to incorporate all these practices into one college class would be a daunting task, but if colleges could work with faculty to incorporate key elements of these models in a consistent instructional methodology, they could develop more learning-centered communities.

While the available models of learning may be valuable in developing a pedagogical framework for faculty members, the already overburdened faculty member in higher education may not be able to review and digest the vast assortment of options (Svinicki, 1990). Implementing some of the current models is also costly. For instance, one costly model is the traditional learning community where groups of students take courses together for a period of one or two years; the curriculum is cross-disciplinary and faculty are trained to team teach as described in Tinto's studies (1999).

This paper will describe a new learning model, "Problem-Based Collaborative Learning", (PBCL), designed to be implemented in a single class and reflecting the combination of many successful elements found in problem-based learning, learning communities and collaborative learning (Krantz, 2004). This model is based on research from five general areas which will be reviewed in the next section.

Review of the Literature

Teacher-Student Relationships

There is a tremendous amount of research examining the relationships between students and teachers and their effect on students' learning. Much of the literature in higher education reflects the virtues of teacher-student relationships (Astin, 1977, 1985, 1993; Bean & Kuh, 1986; Pascarella, 1985; Tinto, 1993). Teacher-student relationships are significant in the building of concrete foundations and structure both academically and socially. It is much like building a house. Built upon a strong foundation, the end result will likely reflect a proud, beautiful house of solid design. Comer (1988) argues that teacher-student relationships constitute essential foundations of the learning process sorely overlooked in educational policy discussion.

Students' responses in emerging research support a significant impact on the learning experience when there is a positive teacher relationship. Caring seems to be a central theme reported by the students. In a study of fifty-four high school students, Phelan (1992) found that students felt that, "teachers who are sensitive and empathetic make a difference in their feelings about school and their ability to achieve academically" (p.428). Additionally, relationships have become an important factor when discussing prominent issues affecting our education system and major problems facing students.

Students appreciate teachers most when they incorporate interpersonal relationships and skills in and out of the classroom. To them the teacher effectively communicating is "real." A substantial body of literature describes the relationship between interpersonal skills and teaching.

Teaching is necessary, interactive, and people centered. Imparting skills, conveying subject content and theoretical concepts, promoting personal development, and building social conscience and responsibility are complex and gradual endeavors requiring regular, close contact between teachers and students. Teaching is not a remote or disengaged activity...[teachers] must cope with the intellectual, physical, social, and psychological complexity of the whole child (Johnson, 1990 p.5).

There is a tremendous amount of research that supports the theory that students benefit from various levels of interpersonal relationships with their teachers. As a general rule, the greater the student-faculty contact both inside and outside the classroom, the greater the promotion of student development and student satisfaction (Astin, 1993). As much has changed in higher education over the past several decades, so has the nature and value of teacher-student interaction (Astin, 1997).

Collaborative Learning

Collaborative learning emphasizes the natural learning that occurs when students are organized into communities where they work together in unstructured groups and create their own learning situations (Johnson, Johnson, & Smith, 1998). Collaborative learning is the use of small groups for instructional purposes. It is not simply putting students in groups to learn; rather, it is structured cooperation among students (Johnson and others, 1991). Its goal is to allow students of different backgrounds and perspectives to work together to maximize learning. In collaborative learning situations, students develop interpersonal relationships through the interdependence and self-evaluation that is representative of group cooperation and conflict. This provides students with the opportunity to share their experiences and backgrounds in the learning process. This sharing leads to learning at a deeper level as they work together to explore new concepts, assimilate new ideas and share prior knowledge. In a meta-analysis of studies relating to student performance through cooperative efforts rather than competitive efforts, cooperative efforts resulted in higher-quality problem solving (Johnson & Johnson, 1994). They concluded that

> *The practical implications of the finding that cooperation generally improves problem solving are obvious. On the job and in the classroom, cooperative groups will be better able to deal with complex problems than will competitors working alone. (p. 140)*

Through the group learning experience supported by these relationships, students develop systems of accountability and responsibility. It is the development of these social skills that will impact the students' readiness to effectively integrate and succeed in today's competitive, global marketplace. Dewey (1938) said that one of the philosophies of education is not to learn merely to acquire information but rather to bring that learning to bear upon everyday actions and behaviors.

Problem-Based Learning

Most educators, as well as institutional goal statements, reflect the need for critical thinking and problem solving skills as crucial to the development of students who can compete in the global market. Problem-based learning utilizes a systematic approach to resolving problems or meeting the challenges encountered in life and the workplace. Problem-based learning is a practical strategy for fostering deeper, critical, active-learning strategies (Ramsden 1992). Boud and Feletti (1991) define problem-based learning as an approach to structuring the curriculum which involves confronting students with problems from practice which provides a stimulus for learning. The recognized history of problem-based learning arose from a desire to provide students with real life scenarios/problems to guide their learning and also to deliver the curriculum as part of a process of critical thinking development (Rhem, 1998). Groups of students set learning objectives and expectations, facilitating student awareness of their own learning needs, students identify potential resources, establish a schedule, research and critique information, and utilize problem—solving methods to explore solutions that will help them with future—related problems (Barrows, 1987).

Working together in problem-based learning situations, students are provided ill-structured problems, a deadline by which they must provide their best solution, and the appropriate curricular information and sources where they can find the information they need in order to make an effective decision. Each week they are provided "twists" in the scenario, and students must react to this new information in determining what course of action to take. Students involved in problem-based learning acquire knowledge in a manner that develops proficiency in problem solving, critical thinking, team participation, and self-directed learning. Through the dynamics of group work and independent investigation, students achieve higher levels of comprehension, develop more learning and knowledge-forming skills and more social skills (Rhem, 1998). Problem-based learning takes account of past experiences, background, and knowledge which can increase students' perceived relevance of curriculum content, stimulate curiosity, and develop essential critical thinking skills ultimately making learning more meaningful (Meyers, 1996; Norman and Schmidt, 1992; Sobral, 1995).

Learning Communities

Tinto (1998) described learning communities as the institutional reorganization of curriculum; whereby, communities are established that enable students to share learning across the curriculum and secondly where faculty reorganize their classrooms to promote shared, collaborative learning experiences. Learning communities exist in many forms, ranging from organizing the curriculum and program for an incoming freshmen class to the connection of a larger global community via electronic media such as the internet or video conferencing. Four or five hundred colleges and universities now offer some form of them, and this number continues to increase (Smith, 2001).

Levine and Tinto have provided descriptions of the many models and characteristics of a learning community, ranging from its simplest form of paired or clustered courses to team-taught courses (Tinto, 1998). The key in any of these formats is that there is some form of positive relationship between the instructor and the student. Learning communities are a broad structural innovation that can address multiple issues from student retention to curricular coherence to faculty vitality for building a greater sense of community (Smith, 2001). Learning communities appear to confront many student and institutional needs including student engagement especially for non-traditional students, student connection and relationship building, sharing of diverse opinions and ideas, shared teaching where faculty members share expertise and ideas, and the appreciation among students for the need to effectively function in a community setting. Tinto's research on the effectiveness of several learning communities at two very different institutions was the first real in-depth study demonstrating the ability of this structure to develop involving and academically challenging environments (Ratcliff & Associates, 1996).

Typically students are asked to work together in groups so that the work of the group cannot be accomplished without each and every member of the group doing their part (Tinto, 1999). Developing a learning community at an institution requires that faculty members have the ability to facilitate learning and to interact effectively with students and colleagues. Teaching in a learning community requires skills, knowledge, and attitudes not necessary in a traditional lecture-style college or university; therefore, faculty must be trained and prepared for the challenge of teaching in learning communities (Oates, 2001). Oates found that collaborative learning and group work are fundamental to learning community practices, and that assignments must be carefully constructed so that faculty takes part in a process of sharing and interacting, rather than each faculty member simply sharing their individual curriculum.

Student Experiences

If colleges and universities are going to move toward a "learning-centered" focus, students must have a stake in helping to improve teaching. One way they are heard is through instructor and course evaluations. Research has demonstrated that student involvement in evaluating teaching, especially when the feedback is accompanied by faculty peer consultation, can help faculty members to improve teaching methods (L'Hommedieu, Menges, & Brinko, 1990). Cooperative student-student interaction and student-teacher interaction are two of the major influences on college effectiveness (Astin,1993) impacting academic and personal development, and satisfaction with the college experience. This satisfaction ultimately leads to greater self-worth, competency development, and the critical thinking ability desired in the workplace. Student participation, teacher support and encouragement and cooperative student interaction lead to positive engagement in critical thinking. (McKeachie, Pintrich, Yi-Guang, and Smith, 1986).

Problem-Based Collaborative Learning Model

The model that will be described in this section incorporates many of the components in the research review that was described in the preceding section. In the problem-based collaborative learning model developed by the authors, the course objectives collectively reflect those of other practitioners utilizing collaborative, problem-based, and traditional learning styles. In this model, however, there is greater flexibility in developing the syllabus and delivering the material. Students take an active role in the learning process by reviewing, evaluating and making recommendations on the structure, goals and expectations outlined in the syllabus. Research consistently demonstrates that students comprehend and retain complex concepts and theories much longer when they are actively involved in their learning process (Light, 1990).

Small communities of students are randomly established within the classroom to facilitate an environment that requires students to learn and exercise effective methods of communicating with their group members (preferably odd numbered groups of 5 to avoid deadlocks). This is done to provide a more realistic experience they might face when entering the workforce. Students remain in the same group for the entire term. Each class period students automatically gather in their groups to review the previous week's material and prepare for the evening's work. This supports the research demonstrating that effective teamwork and collaboration takes time to develop. Michaelsen & Black (1994) found that teams must work together for a substantial amount of time before effective team learning can take place.

Measurement of students' performance includes weekly group assignments consisting of ill-structured problems based on both the concepts covered in the weekly reading assignment as well as additional topics reflecting the importance of the curriculum, communication and group work. These "real life" situations reflect those that students are likely to encounter in their chosen fields of study. The key is not necessarily whether the student groups choose the correct answer or whether they acquire or comprehend the facts presented in the course material. It is more significant that they think critically, utilize research to analyze the presented problem logically, synthesize the information into a workable framework, and apply the appropriate information in choosing a solution. There is more than one reasonable solution based on the application of knowledge and skills rather than one right or wrong answer (Bloom, 1956.)

Students are responsible for completing reading assignments and preparing for the week's topics on their own time. This strategy is based on Claire Weinstein's research in 1988 that reported the benefits of students taking on a greater role in their own learning. She described an undergraduate course where students acquired the knowledge and skills necessary to take more responsibility for their learning. Each time the course was offered, specific goals were set that represented the competencies of goal setting, organization, cognition, and motivation.

In the PBCL model, there may also be a series of quizzes to assess the progress of the students in understanding technical course material. In this model, students take the quiz individually at first. After the quizzes are turned in, the quiz is re-administered to the group to complete together. Doing this enables the instructor to determine where individual students may have deficiencies. It also provides an opportunity for consensus building where the group can compare and contrast knowledge and experience.

In order to give students an opportunity to practice their group work and presentation skills, at the start of each class period, every group is responsible for reading, synthesizing and presenting the information contained in the assigned weekly readings. Students are then evaluated on a prepared evaluation form that reflects their preparation, content, and understanding of the chapter material. Students return to their groups to solve applicable problems based on the curriculum and discussion. The professor is readily available to discuss, elaborate on and interpret the material. Team effort is measured through the use of a peer evaluation where each member of the group has the opportunity to anonymously evaluate the other members of their group based on specific competency categories.

In addition to the weekly assignments, there is a group term project that reflects the discipline and applicability of the course material. This project reflects the competencies necessary to operate effectively both within a group as well as an individual, including

1. Critical Thinking

2. Information Accuracy

3. Clarity of Purpose

4. Product Viability

5. Presentation

6. Recommendations

7. Conducting Research

Each week the instructor spends time developing consecutive stages of team development, coordination and operation. Students are then provided class time to work in their groups and apply these lessons to developing their group term project. It is each group's responsibility to present their findings in a systematic, logical and persuasive manner, where they are able to articulate each step of their research, limitations, analysis, findings, conclusions, and make further recommendations.

Grades and group member participation are general concerns for all students. In order to ensure that each member is recognized for their individual effort, each student must submit a weekly summary of their contribution to the group and project. The group also submits a weekly progress report of its accomplishments reflecting a specific area of the group structure. This provides the professor with a means to determine which students are doing "A" work and which are struggling, so that the professor can identify those needing additional individual or group attention.

Situations can occur where groups fracture, and students come to the instructor stating they cannot work together and want to split up or form a new group. Allowing students to easily disband their group because things are not perfect can be a poor lesson. In the case where this happens, the instructor places the group into a mediation program. Mediation provides an opportunity for the instructor to reinforce the leadership, facilitation and problem solving skills that students will need to be successful in their futures. In rare cases where, despite the mediation program, the group cannot repair the damage, the instructor may have to split the group into smaller groups. In this case, the members understand that the process of creating these new, smaller groups from the original results in lost production time which can then also translate into lower grades.

At the end of the term, each group presents their project to the entire class. This consists of a visual or written research project as well as an oral presentation and facilitated group activity. They present both the positives and negatives of the group experience to ensure a process of self-reflection. Each group member is responsible for presenting a section of the project as well as his or her experiences. Not all students will demonstrate an equal ability to work within and lead group interactions. Because of this, it is possible that some students will not believe they have a chance to excel or even pass the class and they may consider withdrawing. For this reason, all students are provided the opportunity to receive extra credit for their efforts. Extra credit criteria/guidelines are established with class input during the first week of class and may consist of critical participation and demonstrated knowledge of course topics, short papers explaining a course concept or individual experience, or any other piece of information that enriches and contributes to the classroom learning experience.

Another element that can significantly impact students' experience in this model is the commitment of the instructor during non-teaching hours. This time is utilized as an opportunity to initiate informal discussions about the applicability of the course material and a chance to demonstrate to students the tenets of effective communication and true commitment. To this end, office hours are flexible based on the student contacting the professor via e-mail, phone, or in person. A mutually convenient appointment is made much like a business meeting. Students are able to communicate with the professor via the internet, chat room or instant messaging. This demonstrates a commitment to the overall development of the student and is an invaluable means of obtaining student feedback.

Evaluation of the Model

Methodology

In order to determine the effectiveness of PBCL, a study was conducted comparing it to a traditional lecture method. The model was tested at New Jersey City

University, a comprehensive four-year university situated in northern New Jersey, in Autumn, 2002. New Jersey City University offers a variety of liberal arts, education and professional programs leading to both bachelors and masters degrees. The university consists of many non-traditional students including adults, multiple ethnic and cultural backgrounds, and international students). The course utilized in this study introduced students to the management principles of planning, organizing, leading, and controlling. The PBCL model was implemented in a single college class and compared to another class consisting of the same curriculum but based on a traditional lecture model. At the end of the term, students in both the PBCL and lecture classes were asked to voluntarily complete the Student Instructional Report II (SIR II), a questionnaire consisting of 40 Likert Scale survey items. The questions covered the following dimensions.

1.   Supplementary Instructional Methods

2.   Student Effort and Involvement

3.   Communication

4.   Assignments, Exams and Grading

5.   Overall Evaluation

6.   Student Comments

7.   Course Outcomes

8.   Course Organization and Planning

9.   Faculty/Student Interaction

10. Course Difficulty, Workload and Planning

11. Student Information (SIR II, 2002)

The Educational Testing Service (ETS), considered a leader in educational assessment, developed the SIR II, drawing on 30 plus years of proven experience. Centra (1998) identifies the strong relationship between the development of the SIR II and landmark research such as Chickering and Gamson's "Seven Principles For Good Practice In Undergraduate Education"(1987), They also state the need to continue to research and develop active learning methods in order to measure their effect on student engagement as identified by time on task and other effective practices in undergraduate education.

Study Participants

In Class 1, the proposed problem-based collaborative learning model was used as the pedagogical framework for the class. In Class 2, the teaching methodology consisted of a traditional lecture format. In the lecture class, the students' syllabus, course structure, and classroom interaction were presented to them. Lectures reflected the lessons from the chosen textbook, a detailed syllabus outlining course requirements that mirror the text chapters, and the measurement tool reflecting student performance consisted of a midterm and final examination that reflected the content presented in the textbook. The pedagogical belief reflects the more traditional theory that undergraduate college students are mostly uninformed; therefore, learning should reflect the supposition that teacher-student interaction should be based on students' answering questions and asking questions about any material that is not understood. The methodology consisted of lecture, question and answer periods, and class discussions.

Each class shared common objectives based on demonstrating proficiency in specific competencies. As the College of Professional Studies at New Jersey City University utilizes a program of student competencies to measure learning effectiveness, students in both classes were evaluated on their ability to demonstrate a proficiency in critical thinking, oral communication, information literacy and workplace core competencies.

The sample population consisted of 84 students across two class sections. Of the 84 students, 71 fully completed surveys were received and recorded by an independent monitor (Educational Testing Service.) Overall there was an 85% response rate by the entire sample population. In Class 1 (PBCL) there were 35 enrolled students, of which 34 fully completed the survey (a response rate of 97%.) In Class 2 (Lecture) there were 49 students enrolled, of which 37 fully completed the survey (a response rate of 76%.) The data was analyzed through descriptive statistics including calculations of frequencies and percentages to measure experiences and outcomes. T-tests of two independent samples of the two sample populations were also used to determine statistical significance.

Results

Several hypotheses were tested to determine whether the PBCL model would have a significant impact on students' experiences. Significant mean differences were found in the PBCL class over the traditional lecture class in the following evaluated areas.

- student effort and involvement,

- the instructor's communication skills,

- students' experiences,

- students' overall learning,

- students' active involvement in what they were learning,

- class organization and planning,

- the instructor's way of summarizing or emphasizing important points in class,

- problems or questions presented by the instructor for small group discussion,

- term papers or projects,

- laboratory exercises for understanding important course concepts,

- assigned projects in which students worked together, and

- course journals or logs required of students

Further, the results showed a significant difference in the overall evaluation of the PBCL class over the traditional lecture class. The results indicate that the PBCL group perceived the quality of instruction in their class as significantly more effective than the traditional lecture class.

Discussion

PBCL is designed to enrich the experience for the teacher and student. As practitioners, teachers demonstrate an ability to facilitate learning in an atmosphere where students are guided toward effective information absorption and sharing rather than simply being told what the facts are. Students in problem-based learning courses have a more favorable attitude toward their coursework and higher retention rates than those in classes with traditional instruction (Jones, 1996). It is still critical for the teacher to assess the intellectual capital of the students as well as their ability to contribute to the learning process. That is why PBCL includes a commitment to assessing individual student competencies and developing alternative mechanisms to facilitate opportunities to exploit these competencies in the learning process.

Rice and Wilson (1999) stress the societal expectations of collaboration, teamwork, leading, and teaching others. Although most teachers are appreciative of alternative pedagogies and their application in the learning process, few have the resources or time to develop specific, comprehensive models incorporating a specific, consistent method in their classroom. The PBCL can be utilized by a novice or by someone with experience. For faculty feeling the pressure of greater accountability and a demonstration of effective outcomes, PBCL provides specific ways of measuring outcomes and student experiences while maintaining a level of academic freedom demanded by an already burdened faculty.

DeGallow (2003) found that three major complaints from employers about college graduates are their poor communication skills, inability to problem solve, and difficulty working collaboratively with other professionals. Related to these issues is the significant question: Is it necessary for students to understand how they, as future law enforcement officers or doctors, might react when faced with high-risk scenarios? PBCL is designed to provide an opportunity to integrate curriculum with practical experience to address these potential situations both efficiently and effectively. What if law enforcement students were faced with a realistic and solvable "high risk" terrorist scenario? PBCL, used effectively, would provide these students an opportunity to work on solutions with a group of their peers in a classroom setting similar to those they might encounter on the job. The likelihood is that they would enter the workforce with a greater sense of strength and confidence in their team understanding and what their roles might be after this experience rather than having a teacher simply impart the correct answers to them during a lecture. Developing effective solutions as a team using multiple resources, they understand the accomplishment of successfully resolving the situation on their own, hopefully with a minimum or no loss of life or injury.

Recommendations

Problem-based collaborative learning appears to demonstrate how the realities of what students will experience in the workplace can be effectively integrated into the classroom without destroying the integrity of curricular design and delivery. It is more a case of transferring learning from one context to another. There is no one instructional design or pedagogy that will solve all the challenges related to learning and delivery. It is the responsibility of experienced and novice practitioners to continue on a journey of knowledge development and delivery. Because we are unable to predict with certainty the skills needed for the future, it is critical to continue to explore the impact of this and other models of learning. Students must be able to understand and learn how to use their knowledge and critical thinking skills to solve problems and make appropriate decisions. Researchers interested in the achievement of students must develop quantitative and qualitative studies incorporating classroom observations in a variety of contexts. They must be tested in alternative student populations and contexts, whereby the measurement of perceptions and experiences could further shed light on the viability of the methodology. As differences exist, sometimes markedly, between students of different races, ethnicities, socioeconomic status, gender and other backgrounds, further investigation of the impact of teacher perceptions and experiences for various groups are indicated.

Further research could provide greater insight as to how policymakers might develop a comprehensive system of measuring faculty competencies and effectiveness, thereby making a tremendous contribution to the field. Looking at alternative learning models, such as PBCL, leads to an increased understanding of the correlation between student and teacher perceptions as well as the impacts in various settings. Education is effective when students understand the connections and relevance of the subject matter and its application to daily living.

References

Abrami, P., Chamber, B., Poulsen, C., De Simone, d'Appollonia, S., Howden, J. (1995). *Classroom connections: Understanding and using cooperative learning.* Toronto: Harcourt Brace Jovanovich.

Albanese, M. A., & Mitchell, S. (1993). Problem-based curriculum for the preclinical years: A review of literature on its outcomes and implementation issues. *Academic Medicine.* 68 (1), 52-81.

Astin, A.W. (1977). *Four critical years.* San Francisco: Jossey-Bass.

Astin, A.W. (1985). *Achieving educational excellence.* San Francisco: Jossey-Bass.

Astin, A. W. (1993). *What matters in college: Four critical years revisited.* San Francisco: Jossey-Bass.

Astin, A.W. (1997). The changing American college student: Thirty year trends, 1966-1996. *The Review of Higher Education,* 21,115-135.

Bailey, T. (1997). Changes in the nature of work: Implications for skills and assessment. In H.F. O'Neil, Jr. (Ed.), *Workforce readiness: competencies and assessment.* Mahwah, NJ: Lawrence Erlbaum Associates.

Baldwin, Roger G., & Austin, Anne E. (1995). Faculty collaboration in teaching. In Peter Seldin (Ed.), *Improving college teaching.* Bolton, Mass.: Anker.

Banta, Trudy W., Black, Karen E., & Lambert, Jane L. (1999). *Programme assessment for improvement and accountability in the United States.* (Reconsidering quality assurance in higher education: Perspectives on programme assessment and accreditation). Bloemfontein, South Africa: University of the Orange Free State.

Barrows, H. (1987). Learning management in the context of small group problem-based learning. Springfield, IL: Southern Illinois University School of Medicine.

Barr, Robert B., & Tagg, John. (1995 November/December). From teaching to learning: A new paradigm for undergraduate education. *Change Magazine,* 27(6), 12-25.

Bean, J.P. & Kuh, G.D. (1984). The relationship between student-faculty inter-action and undergraduate grade point average. *Research in Higher Education.* 21, 461-477.

Bloom, B. (1956). *Taxonomy of educational objectives. New York: David McKay.*

Bosworth, K. (1995). Caring for others and being cared for: Students talk caring in school. *Phi Delta Kappan,* 76 (9), 686-693.

Boud, D., & Feletti, G.. (1991). *The challenge of problem-based learning.* London: Kogan Page.

Breneman, D. W. & Finney, J. E. (1997). The changing landscape: Higher education finance in the 1990's. In P.M. Callan & J. E. Finney (Eds.), *Public and private financing of higher education: Shaping public policy for the future* (pp. 30-59). Phoenix, AZ: American Council on Education and Oryx Press.

Centra, J.A., Froh, R.C., Gray, P.J., & Lambert, L.M.. (1987). *A guide to evaluation teaching for promotion and tenure.* Action, Mass.: Copley Publishing Group.

Centra, J.A., (1998). *The development of the student instructional report II.* Syracuse University: Educational Testing Service.

Chickering, A.W. & Gamson, Z. F. (1987). *Seven principles for good practice in undergraduate education.* AAHE Bulletin, 39(7). 3-7.

Chickering, A. W., and Gamson, Z.F. (1991). Editor's notes. In A.W. Chickering and Z. F. Gamson (Eds.), *Applying the seven principles for good practice in undergraduate education.* New Directions for Teaching and Learning, 47 (pp.1-3). San Francisco: Jossey-Bass.

Cripe, Edward J. & Mansfield, Richard S. (2002). *The value-added employee.* New York: Butterworth-Heinemann.

Dewey, J. (1938). *Experience and education.* New York: Macmillan.

Feldman, K.A. (1976). Class size and college students' evaluations of teachers and courses: A closer look. *Research in Higher Education,* 1976, 21, 45-115.

Hadwin, Allyson F., & Winne, Phillip H. (1996). Study strategies have meager support: A review with recommendations for implementations. *Journal of Higher Education*, 67, 179.

Haertel, G., & Means, B. (2000). Stronger designs for research on educational uses of technology: Conclusion and implications. *Research Design Papers* Commissioned by SRI International on Behalf of the Office of Technology: U.S. Department of Education.

Halstead, Richard. (1998). Academic success support groups. *Journal of College Student Development*, 39, 507.

Henjum, Arnold. (1983). *Introversion: A misunderstood "individual difference" among students.* ERIC Education 103(1), 39-43. Fall 1982.

Jaworski, Barbara. (1994). *Investigating mathematics teaching: A constructivist enquiry.* London: Falmer Press.

Johnson, D.W., Johnson, R.T., & Smith, K.A. (1991). *Cooperative learning: Increasing college faculty instructional productivity.* Washington, D.C.: The George Washington University, School of Education and Human Development. (ASHE-ERIC Higher Education Reports, No. 4).

Johnson, D. W., & Johnson, R. T. (1994). *Learning together and alone.* Boston: Allyn and Bacon.

Johnson, J., and Farkas, S. (1997). *Getting by: What American teenagers really think about their schools.* New York: Public Agenda.

Johnson, S.M. (1990). *Teachers at work.* New York: Basic Books.

Jones, Diana. (1996). *What is problem based learning?* Retrieved from http://edweb.sdsu.edu/clrit/learningtree/PBL/PBLadvantages.html

Krantz, M. (2004). *An alternative problem-based collaborative learning model and student experiences. Jersey City:* New Jersey City University.

Kuh, G.D., Vesper, N., & Krehbiel, L.E. (1994). Student learning at metropolitan universities. In J.C. Smart (Ed.), *Higher education: Handbook of theory and research*, 10, 1-44. New York: Agathon.

Levine, J. H. (1998). *"Beyond the Definition of Learning Communities"* Metropolitan Universities, 9(1), 11-16.

Light, R. (1990). *The Harvard Assessment Seminars.* Cambridge, MA: Harvard Graduate School of Education.

L'Hommedieu, Randi, Menges, Robert J., & Brinko, Kathleen T. (1990). Methodological explanations for the modest effects of feedback from student ratings. *Journal of Educational Psychology* 82(2).

Matthews, R. (1996). *Learning communities: A retention strategy that serves students and faculty.* Washington, DC: American Association of State Colleges and Universities.

McKeachie, W., Pintrich, P., Yi-Guang, L., & Smith, D. (1986). *Teaching and learning in the college classroom: A review of the research literature.* Ann Arbor, MI.: The Regents of the University of Michigan

Meyers, C. (1986). *Teaching students to think critically: A guide for faculty in all disciplines.* San Francisco: Jossey-Bass.

Michaelsen, L. & Black, R. (1994). *Building learning teams: The key to harnessing the power of small groups in higher education.* In Collaborative Learning: A Sourcebook for Higher Education, 2. State College, PA: National Center for Postsecondary Teaching, Learning and Assessment.

National Board for Professional Teaching Standards.(1998).Retrieved from http://www.nbpts.org/.

Norman, G., & Schmidt, H. (1992).*The psychological basis of problem-based learning.* Academic Medicine 67 (9), 557-565.

Oates, Karen. (2001). Developing the faculty we need. Peer Review (3-4), 9-13. Washington, D.C.: AAC& U.

O'Neil, H.F. Jr. (1999). Perspectives on computer-based performance assessment of problem solving. *Computers in Human Behavior,* 15, 255-268.

Packer, A.(1998). *The end of routine work and the need for a career transcript.* Paper presented at the Hudson Institute's Workforce 2020 Conference, Indianapolis, Indiana.

Pascarella, E.T. (1985). College environment influences on learning and cognitive development: A critical review and synthesis. *Higher Education: Handbook of Theory and Research,*(1), 1-62, New York: Agathon.

Phelan, P., Davidson, A. L., & Cao, H.T. (1992). Speaking up: Students' perspectives on school. *Phi Delta Kappan.* 73 (9), 695-704.

Poplin, M., and Weeres, J. (1994). Voices from the inside: A report on schooling from inside the classroom. *Claremont, CA: Institute for Education in Transformation at the Claremont Graduate School.*

Ratcliff and Associates (1995). *Realizing the potential: Improving postsecondary teaching, learning and assessment.* State College, PA: National Center for Postsecondary Teaching, Learning, and Assessment.

Rhem, James. (1998). Problem based learning: An introduction. Phoenix, AZ:*The National Teaching & Learning Forum,* 8 (1), 1-7.

Rice, M.L., & Wilson, E.K. (1999). How technology aids constructivism in the social studies classroom. *Social Studies* 90 (1), 28-33.

Roeber, Edward. (1995) *Emerging student assessment systems for school reform.* (ERIC Document Reproduction Service No. 389959).

Schroeder, C. C. (2000). *Higher education trends for the next century.* Retrieved from http://Learning Comm\ Collaboration & Partnerships.htm.

Smith, B. L. (2001). The challenge of learning communities as a growing national movement. *Peer Review,* (3-4).4-8.Washington, D.C.: AAC& U.

Sobral, D. T. (1995). The problem-based learning approach as an enhancement factor of personal meaningfulness of learning. *Higher Education Review* 29 (1), 93-101.

Stinson, J.E. & Milter, R.G. (1996). *Problem-based learning in business \ education: Curriculum design and implementation issues.* (New Directions in Teaching and Learning in Higher Education). San Francisco: Jossey-Bass.

Svinicki, Marilla D. (1990). *The Changing Face of College Teaching.* (New Directions for Teaching and Learning, No. 42). San Francisco, CA: Jossey-Bass.

Tinto, V. (1993). *Leaving College: Rethinking the causes and cures of student attrition, 2nd ed.* Chicago: University of Chicago Press.

Tinto, V., Goodsell, A., & Russo, P. (1993). *Gaining a voice: The impact of collaborative learning on student experience in the first year of college.* (Unpublished manuscript). Syracuse, New York: Syracuse University.

Tinto, V. (1998). Colleges as communities: Taking research on student persistence seriously. *The Review of Higher Education*, 21,(2).

Trow, Martin (1973). *The transition from elite to mass to universal higher education (Paper* presented at OECD, Paris, France).

Wehlage, G., Rutter, R., Smith, G., Lesko, N., & Fernandez, R. (1989). *Reducing the risk: Schools as communities of support.* New York: The Falmer Press.

Teaching Physical Comprehension and Exercise Adherence: An Instructional Model

Jan Schlegel

We are changing, we have got to change, and we can no more help it than we can help leaves going yellow and coming loose in the autumn. D.H. Lawrence

Introduction

The incorporation of perception, reasoning and intuition as a basis for developing physical skills may have a positive effect on exercise adherence. Consequently, in order to explore differences in fitness concepts, the individual must access intuition, perception and finally reasoning as a basis for developing movement skills.

Personal experience and exposure to activity become more formalized and comfortable when physical effort is enhanced. Novices, given the opportunity to work at their own pace, will do just that as they are unaware of the hidden potential for greater physical achievement. When a plateau is reached, it must be recognized and evaluated in order to continue to progress as this integration is the basis for personal physical change. This knowledge and awareness clarifies emotional and physical changes as they occur and lessens the potential of either overtraining or getting stuck in the status quo.

Educators of physical disciplines must nurture the process. Enabling the student to trust that the outcome will reflect learned psychomotor skills, which then become an integral aspect of exercise adherence is important. Once a person recognizes a shift in the physical experience, an acceptance of thought patterns which are inherent in questioning the value of activity at the beginning stages seems to diminish.

47

The approach to the activity is now free of preconceived notions concerning the outcome because the students experience joy as a natural extension of their changing psyche and body image; physiological changes become more recognizable and acceptable to the participant. Reflection of the experience brings clarity of purpose as physical changes become more apparent; consequently, continuous exercise patterns become more desirable.

Learning Challenges

(This section is enhanced by the words of students who have experienced the challenges described in the author's text.)

The same methods that were used to get us in shape in the beginning stages of conditioning were preparing us for competition. We had no idea that teaching technique would make the transition to using free weights easier.

The self-assessment helped by allowing me to look back and see what I was doing wrong or right technically. It was good to let out my feelings about the workout.

It is important that we, as educators, recognize the challenges which may be experienced during the process of learning. Establishing and focusing on the purpose of intention as well as setting goals may help clarify the outcome. During the journey to the final destination, there may be many variables which we must be willing to accept, trust and refine in order to reach our final destination. Students may become frightened of the psychophysical changes which they may experience along the way. These may cause them to veer off course or possibly create a diversion that detracts from the original intention at which point a decision to forgo the original quest for exercise adherence is in danger of being lost.

There were a few times when I felt like I was questioning why I was doing this, thinking that everything I was learning would never be put to use. It was alright that I knew I could lift a lot of weight, but will anyone else know this?

My arms were burning and aching inside. After the pushups I felt shaky. I think it was because all the weight was on my arms. I will never do them again because I would not like to have bulky arms; also the pain in my arms was too intense.

The goal has changed because the course of action has changed, creating evidence which indicates that it may be inappropriate to meet the original goal. Physical comprehension which directly relates to exercise adherence has broken down in the absence of knowledge. This process may also be a direct effect of the readiness factor where distractions become fodder for feelings of incompetence; thus, confidence wanes.

This was my first experience working out in the pool. I am not a swimmer.

My attitude towards exercising on a daily basis has to grow, but it is still easy for me to be side tracked or to find excuses.

I was shy about getting on the machines in the fitness center, especially the ones I had no clue about.

I don't know if I'll make it in tomorrow. I hadn't done any exercises in a week, and yesterday was intense. I'm thinking of changing my workout days. I want to do this, but it is the second time in a row that something bad happened. It could be just a coincidence, but I'd rather do less. I'm not bailing out, I want to do it, but I have the rest of my life, so what's the rush? I don't want to get discouraged and give up because I'm overtraining.

The above student had developed an amazing self—motivated plan to change his dietary lifestyle habits with much success but adding an exercise component to his regime became a real challenge. The heart was there, but the body was having a hard time experiencing intense changes in the exercise format. He worked through his ups and downs with the support of a partner, e-mails and personal sessions. He tried but was unable to give himself the permission needed to enjoy the physical changes his body was experiencing even after receiving an excellent physical report from his personal physician.

It is up to the teacher to filter out the feelings of self-doubt by offering students a variety of approaches to physical activity. This will allow for re-entry into the physical application of exercise while students explore personal comfort zones and balance extremes. Having the opportunity then to make choices based on emotional response to exercise is a valid concern and one that must not be overlooked. Giving students this freedom of choice, will help them to recognize and value personal commitment. Physical and emotional consciousness then offers an opportunity to make knowledgeable decisions about personal growth and development.

It has been said that a person's mental state plays a significant role in the success of physical performance.

The teacher helped me get a better grasp on what we were learning by demonstrating positions, showing common errors and how to avoid making them, and by using proper execution in technique. It was very thorough and repeated until everyone was comfortable with learning. Answers were clear, unambiguous, and the teacher had a refreshing sense of humor which made the experience more enjoyable.

The assessment sheet also allowed me to be more open-minded while thinking about areas of improvement. This helped me to monitor my progress and stay on track with my goals.

There are rules which are important to aerobic or anaerobic training in order for the experience to be more beneficial and develop exercise compliance. The physiological and psychomotor aspect of any activity which is applied through scientific research does not have to be presented in a fashion that could alienate new students. An awareness of simple behavioral techniques is beneficial for beginning students since they are undoubtedly going to encounter new bodily sensations when starting a physical activity.

In doing high pulls, I have to improve my speed. I learned that speed is the key in doing the pull correctly. I must go slow, and after I get above the knee quickly increase my speed while pulling the bar up.

In the power pull, I learned that I should use my legs rather than my arms in pulling the bar up. One of my strengths is my legs and, in doing cleans, my strength was speed. I was able to get under the bar pretty quickly.

It was a great experience to learn something I would never think twice about doing especially from a girl's point of view. I think that I am a completely different person now then I was in the beginning of the semester.

I really impressed myself with the weight I lifted because I never thought I could do that much and I learned that proper positioning is important when executing an exercise.

It is of utmost importance for the person to feel safe while in a state of uncertainty and to be able to accept the initial feeling of not being in total physical control. It involves an openness to the new physical sensations they are about to experience and also to the changes they are about to encounter. Kinesthetic movement sensation involves body position, balance or movement which is stimulated by the nerves to the musculoskeletal system. Thus having a mirror in the form of a teacher, trainer or friend who is knowledgeable and supportive in the fitness area is appropriate at the beginning stages of exercise adherence.

The beginning is an exciting place to be in the journey to fitness. With the learner's mind open to the vast array of possibilities which might occur over time, it is up to physical educators to create an unthreatening environment in which the novice can build a foundation of understanding while also enjoying the physical sensations which are about to unfold.

Doing the write up after class did help develop my technique because I could see improvement from my previous entry. This was motivating since I knew I had overcome an obstacle in lifting and would know what needed to be worked on next. It helped me to look at my strengths and weak points.

I enjoyed taking this class. When we started a few weeks ago I did not know what to expect. Taking this course helped me to grow both physically and mentally. Physically because I'm stronger then when I started and mentally in that I was exposed to something totally new and learned to perform certain movements correctly while understanding more about anatomy and power.

By choosing to experience fitness, students will enhance their emotional stability and physical prowess. They will develop the potential to experience health, happiness and mental clarity by simply learning how to care for themselves through life's physical journey.

All we as educators can offer our students is the learning environment. We can invite them in to experience as much as they are willing to comprehend, and we must be prepared to offer a variety of choices for further development. We, as educators, must feel committed to our students' personal learning processes and put less emphasis on how the learning takes place in general. When students have a thirst for knowledge, teachers are given the gift of furthering their own personal growth at the same time.

Continuously challenging the students to explore new concepts will then personalize the learning process. It is up to us to have the pallet ready in order to offer students a variety and range of colors on the canvas of experience.

Readiness is a factor in the learning exchange, and it is the task of the teacher to create the environment which will encourage thinking and engage students to open up to the thought process that will lead them towards the desire for greater knowledge. It is a kind of puzzle which has no absolute pattern as each student has a very individual pattern of physical comprehension.

The teacher simply offers the information without the sense of owning the outcome although it will reflect an end product which has wonderful variations based on the differences of the students' interpretations and personal expressions.

But then I did one lift where my chest and body were up before I moved down under the bar, and I did it perfectly. After that I moved up in weight pretty fast, and I felt that my technique is more successful now.

My assessment of my performance is that I have progressed because I am using the proper technique. I will do more reps with less weight to practice what I am doing incorrectly. When I fixed my technique, I added more weight. I grew because I realized what I was doing wrong and fixed it. Realizing that if I put my mind to something, I can do it helps me to strive for a better performance.

I enjoyed this class when I learned that we would actually be doing the exercises we were reading about.

To help the students visualize each lift we were introduced to a website to supplement what was being taught. It explained proper execution and preparation for the movements we were learning. As the weeks passed we could see our progress.

I wrote down what I actually did during the class sessions and how I felt during the lifts. Writing down what I thought I did incorrectly helped me to review my form and this helped me understand where I stood on an individual basis. At no time did I feel as if I was competing with other classmates. I watched myself grow stronger throughout the semester.

Structured Improvisation in the Teaching Approach and Setting Limits

Accessing learning curves based on critical thinking is an important aspect of the process which helps to develop the ability to set realistic goals. This enables students to adapt to the assessment tools effectively in order to help them personally monitor fitness goals as they relate to specific activities. A continuum of goals must be set up in order to monitor physical changes realistically while they are occurring during a program of exercise. This will enable students to recognize personal achievements based on their training habits while honing skills which will also support proper biomechanics needed to successfully endure more intense workout regimes. In order to access a healthier lifestyle, fitness and exercise must be integrated with consistency as an automatic aspect of everyday life.

In the area of fitness and exercise, we must be able to address recognizable physical competencies and access strategies which help develop strengths and address weaknesses within the body mechanics. This approach may require the use of inherently tactile experiences which are movement based and taught through a variety of physical disciplines.

Each skill is taught as a process having within its framework components of the whole which are practiced in sequences and at different levels of success. The disciplines include setting goals, commitment to practice, recognizing the value of consistency, changes in achievement levels, and variables in exercise format which take into consideration age, gender, overall health and anatomical differences. Change is thus reached at different levels on a continuum. Success then becomes a more personalized experience for the learner.

> *As the weeks passed, we could see our progress as we continued learning new movements associated with the technique being practiced. We were then able to put the movements together to perform the lifts perfectly.*

> *To give us an idea of why individuals choose to train, a video of a junior national's competition was shown in class. This helped us recognize the importance of training and the value of performing a skill proficiently. Competitors don't want to be thinking about the mechanism of the lifts, they just want to execute the moves to the best of their ability.*

> *My initial reaction to the class was frustration. We were doing all these different workouts regardless of the shape we were in. I thought it was a little crazy, but I started getting into it and actually enjoyed doing it. I learned a lot and really enjoyed the class.*

> *Things get easier once you have the momentum going; it's just the first few movements that seem to be the hardest. Working out at first was a bummer for me, but once I was into it, I looked forward to doing it.*

> *I found out that a lack of sleep prior to a workout makes it more difficult to get through the work compared to not eating properly although both set a person up at a disadvantage.*

The Value of Change

Most of us believe we want to change—to improve ourselves—but our Basic Self needs boundaries, thrives on limits, and remains fond of familiar patterns. We carry the weight of inertia, the resistance to change, within us. (Millman, 1992, p.94)

Change involves movement into unknown territory; if we are open to it we find the experience less threatening. When we become receptive to learning while in the process of change, patterns of thought, clarification of concepts and motor learning are all potentially affected through the clarification of facts. This process then allows for the patience needed in facing the difficulties which might surface when faced with a new physical task. Students then experience the challenge of preparation which is an integral part of the growth process. By understanding basic fears and concerns they potentially face when experiencing something new, students can develop the patience and insight needed to confront the task which opens the mind to new patterns of learning. The experience of change gets easier knowing that practice is a necessary component of success if we apply ourselves.

> *I never stayed on the Stairmaster for a long period of time. I always gave up and went to something else. I have grown because I actually liked feeling the results the next day although initially my attitude was horrible because I didn't want to do the workout. I realized that if I was able to stay on the machine for that long that I will try to continue working on it.*

Change involves giving up a part of our consciousness, our pattern of security; it is a trade off when we give up something we want for something we want more. It is neither good nor bad; thus, judgments should not reflect the outcome. Focusing on the benefits of what might be gained rather than what we are giving up, is one approach in experiencing clarity and creating success. Setting personal goals which are meaningful, combined with the reality of reaching some level of success, will open the door to a positive learning outcome.

The individual perception of the benefits of change may not be enough fuel to create motivation. Students may find it necessary to work with systems of rewards, either self-motivated or grade—oriented, as a means to an outcome appropriate to support change. The learner becomes more secure in the self as the reward is a subconscious compensation for success which is associated with change and pleasure.

> *I came to this class with the expectation that I was going to learn how to work out and learn about basic nutrition. Instead, I came away with more than I ever expected. I learned why water is so important to a healthy diet. I also learned about new exercise formats in the weight room which all helped me to lose forty pounds.*

> *I tried something different. Instead of lifting, I tried step aerobics, spinning, stretching and interval training on the treadmill. This taught me that there is more to becoming physically fit than just lifting weights. All aspects of fitness must*

be incorporated, and giving up is not an option if you are to experience success. I tried different things, and gave myself a chance to learn something new, it didn't come easily, but I was successful.

Students understand basic concepts through kinesthetic feelings and direct experience. Goal—oriented lessons are best taught then through movement patterns in an applied physical setting. Integrating the concept of mental resistance with learning becomes clear while experiencing physical resistance; the application is easily transferred from the body to the mind within the physical setting. Lifting weight in a strength training session or experiencing aerobics while practicing longer, faster time sets may enhance the physical challenge which reflects growth and physical change on many levels.

It was something new to me, and I had a hard time trying to do it, to get it right, because I never did it before. I wasn't worried because I knew that I liked what I was doing and that this was a new challenge. It took time for me to get used to the technique. It wasn't hard. It was just that I had to get the correct form. It's important to use your mind in order to understand a new physical movement. It then becomes easier.

It was crazy but I got the hang of it, and I became better at it. I learned so much from how to count in kilograms to recognizing the differences in equipment.

I learned a lot because the teacher helped me. The class was fun, and everybody tried their best. We competed against each other in the friendliest, most supportive way at the end of the semester, and everything we learned came together in competition.

I was very impressed with my classmates. We have practiced hard throughout the semester, and it was time to see the results. The girls were first, and I was there to support them. They impressed me the most; they were lifting more weight than expected and with flawless technique.

The focus changed, and I was not as concerned with getting a good grade as I was with performing well on the platform. This made coming to class fun at this point because I was focused. I had a goal, and I knew the objectives in obtaining that goal. To work so hard all semester, to get to this point was well worth it.

During the final competition, it is easy to see why it is so important to be properly trained. This is when we expect the body to perform the lifts naturally with little thought, and I felt that my body was ready to perform the movements exactly as I trained during class.

Physical comprehension, reasoning and intuition can be used as a base for developing physical skills which challenge and explore a variety of fitness concepts. Personal qualities which are developed through physical activities include mental focus, emotional energy, plus the ability to relax the mind/body in stressful situations. Offering learning situations to students with varied backgrounds becomes a challenge. In these situations, teaching self-awareness techniques serves as a tool to support self-sufficient learners. This allows students to recognize their position relative to their goal and establishes a means to a more personal approach to development. Students then have an opportunity to recognize the value of changing goals because they understand that it is a reflection of personal advancement which supports individual growth patterns and creates a vision based on conviction and potential.

There are a variety of physiological components which characterize performance and impact both the mental and physical comprehension of a skill. The skill level involved in the ability to adhere to exercise is affected by this phenomenon. Exploring, sharing and understanding these concepts may help to eliminate some of the doubts, fears, and beliefs which beginners usually experience while attempting new physical task levels.

> *I was weak and extremely stiff before the exercises due to my iron deficiency, but the exercise often stimulated me. I felt determined to try to do each exercise at least once. There was one skill that was definitely out of my league, but I tried it. I was physically sore and mentally scared to death. I kept imaging that I would stumble and fall. I survived although I was sore the next day, but it was a good soreness, and I knew it was beneficial to my growth. My exercising on a daily basis might be possible after all.*

Skill Acquisition and Proficiency: Skilled versus Novice Performers

Guthrie (1952) defines a skill as the ability to bring about some end result with maximum certainty and minimal outlay of energy or time and energy. A novice could conceivably execute a flawless motor skill, yet not be able to perform it consistently.

Consistency rather than execution of new motor skills which may be performed with little effort becomes a challenge to the novice; it is at this juncture that emotional support becomes appropriate while offering corrections which relate to the performance of the task at hand. Distractions will prevail if students feel judged either by themselves or by the onlooker. This is a very volatile situation for both parties if the aim is perfection of the skill rather than the integration of the skill into psychophysical adaptation.

> *I felt safe and confident in what I was doing and learning, but I have to admit I was a little afraid of what the teacher might say, but the corrections weren't about me. They were about the technique I was learning so it became easier to listen to both the negative and positive criticism.*

Since an individual is limited to performing one complete task at a time (Boutcher, 1993), an individual may have to divert all of their attentional capacity toward a new task. As individuals practice a particular motor skill, they eventually learn to eliminate extraneous movement and to effectively coordinate muscles to act as a single functional unit. As skills become automatic considerably less thought is necessary to effectively complete the task.

> *The memories of the first class were that I was sore, and I did not think I would get the technique down. When class began with strength training and conditioning, my body was not used to working out. I would say the hardest part of this class was that I would think too much, and that made the activity feel worse.*

> *Addressing exercise issues as well as nutritional changes, my experience in the last five months enhanced my success. Self—motivation came from the learning experience. With the support and knowledge I received while training, this allowed me to believe in myself. Every week I felt my self—esteem growing stronger. The intense combination of nutritional and exercise programming changed my life.*

Behavioral Perspective

A behavioral perspective suggests that we can facilitate the development of performance by changing the environment. This may be accomplished by the application of specific stimulus in a systematic manner as in social reinforcement, praise or disapproval. When the stimulus (psyche) and skill (physical task) support each other, this association may strengthen potential goal setting. Focusing on a desired outcome then enables proficiency to be monitored through observation which may enhance behavior.

> *The cardio training course was very helpful to me because it encouraged me to continue working out in my free time. It was because the professor was very down to earth, and took the time to personally teach us the skills.*

I liked the class because it helped me to improve my physical condition while I learned about the different changes my body goes through when I exercise.

I was very happy with the way the course was taught, and the progress I made. The variety of exercises and activities that were done in class helped me tremendously in achieving my personal fitness goals. I wish more instructors were like my professor whose knowledge, expertise, personality and attitude towards students was most helpful.

I really enjoyed the fitness class. I learned a lot of new activities and different exercises which inspired me to continue on my own.

Cognitive/Behavioral Perspective

The cognitive/behavioral approach takes into consideration an individual's thought process. Recognizing the importance of individual belief systems and memories may create a bias which can negatively affect the development of skill proficiency. Teaching students to recognize specific cues while performing a motor skill may support their success and therefore change initial beliefs related to the task. Proficiency is monitored by self-report within the cognitive/behavioral approach. Interestingly, experienced performers know what it feels like to perform their particular motor skill yet often have difficulty in articulating their actions and perceptions verbally. Information is thought to be lost when explaining a skill or tacit knowledge; furthermore, automatic processing of a motor skill appears free of conscious monitoring. (Boucher, 1992)

I want to be able to do this skill effortlessly, like second nature. I'm anxious to get it right. Just knowing that I can make my body do it will give me the confidence I need to improve my technique.

I need to watch and remember my hand positioning on the bar, recording on paper where my hands should be positioned may help me. I know that repeating the lifts over and over again will enhance my personal growth because of the practice. I know that I can make my body do things that I never expected it to do; this is part of having the right attitude.

Watching the video feedback let me see my movement. I also paid attention to constructive criticism.

The self—assessments after each session didn't help my technique because I didn't take the time to internalize what happened physically. I used the writing more as a reflection than a device to help my technique. I felt that the video feedback helped me more because I saw myself physically doing the work and therefore saw where I needed to improve. Watching the video made the greatest impact on my technique.

I'm a visual learner, not to say that I can't read something and internalize it, but watching skills performed in front of my eyes is more effective. I can pick up the *movements much more quickly with a visual approach.*

When novice performers are in competitive situations, they attempt to consciously monitor the process of performance. Unfortunately, conscious or control processing does not contain the necessary information for optimal muscular coordination essential for effective performance. (Boutcher,1993)

I know I snatched the 35 kilo weight correctly, but it was just too heavy for me. But it felt really good to get the 32 kilo snatch up in front of everybody.

I could have lifted a lot more weight in the competition if I spent more time practicing out of class. I am pretty confident that my form is good; however, I am nervous about snatching and squatting at the same time because I have to work on my speed.

We were going to be judged on technique by real judges. This added pressure to the situation. I was excited and scared to death at the same time. Everyone was nervous, but I think we surprised ourselves. It was fun, and I learned a lot.

Being judged by a former Olympic weightlifter was some experience; I had to calm my nerves. I was really nervous after watching the first few lifters. This physical final was a great challenge, and all the students became very serious about their performances.

There are a variety of physiological components which affect physical performance. This may have a psychological impact on the person attempting to integrate physical activities into their lifestyles as the benefits are not immediately accessible without commitment to the unknown. This may include sensations of pain which is involved in the recovery process and in the beginning stages of exercising. Often the participant is unable to rationalize this. Understanding these concepts may help to eliminate some of the doubts, fears and misconceptions usually experienced initially when accepting the physical sensations of learning a physical activity.

I learned the importance of stretching as a warm-up and cool-down routine. First I was complaining about the pain, but now I like stretching. I have more flexibility and I believe it will improve my overall fitness.

The most valuable insight I learned was that the longer I continue to workout the better I become at it. *In the beginning my muscles ached and tired quickly. Now I work out for up to twenty minutes before the first real signs of discomfort, and I am able to push myself through the initial aches. This is really great.*

By doing other exercises that will increase power in my legs, I was able to last longer on the treadmill. Although it took a lot out of me physically I am now able to recognize and tolerate more discomfort during the workout. It's alright to feel tired because exercise takes a lot out of you. I now feel that I have strength in my body.

Pain tolerance during recovery may add or detract from the original desire to continue activities which might be perceived as the cause of the discomfort. Monitoring physical output with consideration for personal fitness levels becomes an invaluable tool for the newly motivated participant. It is important to monitor the process and instill a sense that participation and patience is significant. Experiencing the outcome of overloading the system too soon may be painful and thus discouraging. It is important that the student learn to recognize the value of moderation at the onset of an exercise program. Executing the appropriate warm-up, duration and intensity of an activity gives the body a chance to respond as the psyche recognizes and learns to accept the physical discomforts which are appropriate to exercise intensity. The mind/body continuum will then reap the benefits of health and wellbeing which can only be reached through physical effort.

If we focus on behavioral goals while experiencing exercise the student is given the opportunity to recognize physical patterns as they relate to specific physical sensations. Recognizing these training effects due to changes in physical behavior could enhance the initial experience. Endurance, stamina, and strength, while being developed, will support the physical comprehension needed to achieve the outcome which is a greater understanding of the process.

The more control the student experiences during exercise the greater impact it will have on the learning experience and the benefits of the exercise. Achieving and recognizing goals allows students to be personally involved in their physical outcomes.

Exercise involves the perception of movement through self-directed learning. The joy of movement, in essence, is an emotional experience which is very per-

sonal; any rationale for performing a physical task must be perceived as potentially valuable to the participant. Physical compliance may reflect a commitment
to exercise based on the physical sensations being perceived by the student as beneficial to a student's self image. This creates a more personal connection to the
changes which are being developed within them through applied fitness.

> *I enjoyed this activity because I pushed myself to a point that I did not know
> existed. I was physically and mentally tired in the end.*

> *In the spinning class experience, I enjoyed the idea of not knowing what to expect
> but was very delighted in the end.*

> *I kept walking and running even though my legs were tired. I had a positive atti-
> tude and was happy and looked forward to the exercise. I find that I can push
> myself a little more and feel great after the workout.*

> *Before this course, my main motivation for working out was vanity; however, since
> I started the independent study I became more aware of the importance of my
> health and how the foods I eat affect my system. Because of this experience, I
> became more serious about my diet and realized the significant effect of proper diet
> on my desired fitness goals.*

We pay a price for movement or the lack of it from infancy to adulthood.
Mobility is a precious commodity as it allows for the freedom of self-sufficiency.
Our society reveres those who enjoy the physical sensations of the body in
motion during dance, athletics, organized sports competitions or personal physical challenges. Yet there are those individuals whose perceptions of themselves are
simply nullified by the simplest physical task. It then becomes the charge of the
physical educator to support this learning.

Final thoughts, questions and reflections

Why do some simply exercise while others who try get side tracked by wanting to
know the value in it first? What is it that we value in the physical or the mental
task? Pushing through the pain/pleasure threshold at extremes of physical performance, be it the novice or athlete, all face a daunting task. The Special Olympics
challenges the simplicity of the action. Simply the willingness to try becomes
enough to create success. Why do we return to an event or activity, after trying
and/or failing to reach a projected outcome? Why must we try again? Do we
value some aspect of the activity or is it the challenge? Discussing these concepts

with students may create an awareness of the changes which are possible in both our mental and physical comprehension during exercise training.

Life is movement; death is lack of movement, and neither has a goal attached to the outcome. The body has systems which function to help support movement. Although this is taken for granted by many, there are those who respect and/or challenge the system along life's journey.

What makes the difference in the approach to accepting a new experience and incorporating it into a lifestyle? Is it the goal one wishes to attempt to reach or is it simply the path to that goal which may include positive health changes and therefore fitness adherence?

First, we must experience the desire to change; we must intuitively realize the value in this process. Second, finding the means to the goal which brings the best possible results is paramount to continuing the quest, or we find ourselves simply giving up questioning the value of the task itself. The way to fuel the passion for physical exercise adherence is to create the environment for change.

There is a difference in the intensity of the commitment as it relates to training versus a lifelong fitness goal, and both indicate great fortitude. Happiness is a cornerstone of both as we find people decreasing their commitment when they begin to put qualifiers on the outcomes. Change takes place when we are ready to accept the process with an understanding and patience that allows the process to unfold naturally. Harsh judgments, impatience or predictions as to what should, or should not, be occurring in our physical experience only gets in the way of performance.

There is a maturity needed in order to maintain the changes required along the way. Exercise and diet must be embraced with a youthful exuberance as we travel on this incredible journey. Only when they are present, will we be open to change both physically and mentally both of which are key elements that allow us to integrate fitness into our lives and to open the door to physical comprehension and exercise adherence.

References

Apples, Dan (2000). *Learning Assessment Journal.* 4th edition, 53, 67, Pacific Crest.

Boutcher, S.H. (1993). On the affective benefits of acute aerobic exercise: Taking stock after twenty years of research. In P. Seraganian (Ed.), *Exercise psychology: The influence of physical exercise on psychological processes.* New York: Wiley.

Guthrie, E.R.. (1952). *The Psychology of Learning,* revised edition. Peter Smith Pub. Inc..

Millman, Dan (1992). *No ordinary moments.* H.J. Kramer Inc.

Acknowledgments

I would like to acknowledge the following individuals for their help in writing this article.

Dr. Karyn Marshall, a female world champion athlete in Olympic weightlifting,

Dr. Michael Mahoney, PhD. (Distinguished Professor of Psychology) and an Olympic weightlifter,

Mark Cohen, a respected Olympic weightlifting coach, personal trainer/teacher, and

My N.J.C.U. fitness students, Spring, 2004.

The Question is the Answer

Rosalyn D. Young, Esq.

Introduction

Here is a question. What traits do critical thinkers, creative thinkers and active learners have in common?

In a recent faculty workshop with faculty teaching Civilization I at New Jersey City University, faculty participants were asked to identify the cognitive and affective traits common to both critical and creative thinking. Among the traits they listed were: open mindedness, curious, willing to play with new ideas, risk-takers, "thinking outside the box", self-aware, constructing own knowledge, and relating new ideas to existing knowledge. I think we would agree that these are some of the traits that we as faculty hope to instill and develop in students with active learning (also referred to as "student-centered learning") pedagogies. We want our students to be engaged in learning, to be active (rather than passive) learners, to develop self-awareness, to develop their own informed judgments about the world, and to be receptive to new ideas. We want our students to continually *construct* their own knowledge by utilizing their creativity and critical thinking skills (really two sides of the same coin—although that's for another discussion).

Underlying the ability to think critically and creatively, and a precondition for active learning, is the desire and ability to ask questions. As learners and educators, we are masters at asking questions. We therefore often fail to appreciate the difficulty our students have in generating questions, for example, to fill in gaps in information, to discover relationships, to challenge what they are learning, to explore how the pieces fit together, to evaluate alternatives, to form value judgments, and to import knowledge from other contexts. Although I have been teaching college students for over ten years, I am continually amazed at how little skill (and willingness) students have in generating questions. And without the desire and ability to continually ask questions, neither critical thinking nor creative thinking are possible. Lacking the ability (and willingness) to ask questions, students remain passive learners—merely receptacles for the information transferred from us to them in the classroom.

So how do we help students to develop good questioning skills? And how do we encourage students to develop good questioning *habits*? This paper will discuss three different pedagogies that can help students improve their ability to ask good questions and make their question-asking habitual.

The Question Rubric

In the text I use for my Critical Thinking course, *Critical Thinking, Thoughtful Writing* (Houghton Mifflin, 2004), John Chaffee (in a chapter on *Creative Writing)* classifies questions into six categories: Fact, Interpretation, Analysis, Synthesis, Evaluation, and Application (paralleling Bloom's taxonomy), and provides question stems for each type. (Alternatively, a hand-out with this information could be used). We start off by reading an article about some controversial issue that I think my students will find interesting and I then ask them to prepare six questions (one from each of Chaffee's categories and using the question stems to help them) about the article. This leads to a discussion of the differences between a "good" and "poor" question, which is then turned into a "Question Rubric". Students are usually amazed at how poor their initial questions are (typically asking for information that is in the article already or irrelevant to the issue in the article) when evaluated applying the criteria of the Question Rubric. Students are also perplexed at how difficult they find it to come up with good questions, particularly the "higher order" ones beyond the basic *who, what, where, when,* and *how* types.

I generally give my students one article a week (or use an article selected by a student) for this exercise, and continue to discuss different aspects of good questioning skills, and the importance of developing questions of each type (to reflect the different ways that we process information). As students progress in their question-asking skills, they improve particularly in their ability to develop questions from the "higher order" thinking skills (e.g., questions of application and evaluation).

I find that the students are more enthusiastic and "buy-in" more easily if they participate in developing the Question Rubric used during the semester so I resist just handing out the one my previous class developed. It also gives us a better opportunity to discuss each of the elements and gauge their importance. With some subtle guidance from me, however, the rubric invariably covers the essential traits we need to focus on during the semester. A sample of the Question Rubric is attached at the end of this paper so the discussion about it will be brief.

The first four criteria of the Question Rubric relate to advancing the student's understanding of the article (although it can be used with any type of reading or even oral presentation). A good question (or a set of questions) must be relevant to the issues being raised rather than focus on unimportant issues. I find students often miss the issue that surrounds the controversy, and ask questions about irrelevant and/or unimportant issues. A good question needs to seek important information that will enhance the questioner's understanding of the issue. I find students often ask questions that are already answered in the article. A good question is also one that will help the questioner reflect on his/her own experiences and be personally meaningful. Interestingly, this attribute was suggested by my students and was not one I had originally thought of including in the rubric. It is also one of the hardest criteria to meet, since it requires students to relate the issues in the article to their personal values.

The last three criteria of the Question Rubric relate to the students' clarity of thinking and ability to express their ideas clearly, and grammatically (their English teacher appreciates this). Finally, the students need to utilize questions from each category and be able to appropriately categorize them.

The Question Rubric can also be used in peer—to—peer reviews and group activities. A student can present his/her questions to the entire class and generate a class discussion, or students can work in smaller groups, evaluating and improving each other's work. Questioning contests can also be constructed by allocating points to each criteria in the Rubric (so for example, relevance, information and purpose may each be worth 2 points and the remaining elements 1 point each) and then having each group compete (judged by me or another group of students) for the most points with their group's questions.

In one semester, most students in my Critical Thinking class do show improvement in their questioning skills. With the early articles, students tend to ask questions that focus on irrelevant issues or whose answers are already contained in the article. In addition, their questions tend to be poorly constructed and vague. By the end of the semester, students' questions are more focused and relevant to the controversial issue contained in the article, and contain more sophisticated "higher order" application and evaluation questions.

For example, one student's question early in the semester about an article dealing with keeping sex offenders in jail after their terms were up, asked: "Why does the State allow the diagnosis be framed by law makers instead of the doctors who should be evaluating the patients?". His other questions were similarly unfocused, repetitive (asking for the same facts with different formulations) missed entirely the controversial issues discussed in the article (such as the civil right concerns over incarcerating people for their thoughts, and the lack of due process in the commitment proceedings), and failed to explore any alternatives to indefinite incarceration. The same student at the end of the semester about an article dealing with surveillance cameras in the classrooms in a Biloxi Mississippi school, asked a number of well-framed, thoughtful, and relevant questions, such as: "What are the percentage of schools in the United States which are equipped with surveillance cameras in the classroom?" (*Fact*); "What is the rate of crime or wrong doings in schools equipped with cameras compared to those schools that are not equipped? (*Interpretation*); "Do the students feel that their rights of privacy are being taken away because of the constant watch over them? (*Analysis*). Not only did these questions focus on the main controversial issues, they each sought additional relevant information in order to frame a more educated opinion about the issues. Another student who began the semester with extremely, poor questions, showed marked improvement by the end of the semester. For an article dealing with California's 3-Strikes Law (in which petty offenses can lead to a life sentence), the student asked: "How is the three strikes law an example of helping rid the streets of violent criminals when you are releasing rape offenders and murderers before shoplifters who steal video tapes three times? (*Application*). And in the same vein: "How can you decide on releasing a one-time offender who was carrying a pound and a half of cocaine but keeping a shoplifter in jail for life? (*Evaluation*). Although obviously these questions could be refined, they do indicate improvement in the student's critical thinking skills.

I asked my students in my Critical Thinking class at the end of the semester what benefits, if any, they believed they personally derived from the questioning pedagogy used throughout the course. Not only did the students believe they had improved their question-asking skills, they also felt that they had developed the *habit* of asking questions in their other courses as well, which improved their understanding of the course material and even made the course more interesting to them.

FIRAC

I have been teaching Business Law for over ten years. I recognized early on in my teaching of this course that with its emphasis on problem solving and inquiry orientation, it was a natural vehicle for helping students develop critical thinking skills (when taught in an active learning environment). By having students apply legal concepts and principles to critically analyze legal problems and develop solutions (rather than passively learn/memorize those same concepts and principles) students are required to actively (and creatively) employ each of Bloom's thinking skills, from the "lower order" factual thinking skills to the "higher order" evaluation and application skills.

One pedagogy used in law schools to help students analyze and develop solutions for legal problems called *IRAC* adapted quite easily to a Business Law college-level course. Adding the *F* to emphasize the importance of identifying the relevant *Facts* in any legal issue, *FIRAC* stands for: Facts, Issue, Rule, Application (and/or analysis or argument depending on the context), and Conclusion. Students are often asked to "think critically" in college but are not given any actual guidance or methodology to accomplish this.

FIRAC provides such guidance by providing a step-by-step methodology to be used in analyzing legal problems. And embedded in the entire *FIRAC* methodology, is the process of asking of good questions.

First the *Facts.* Although a simple concept (and despite being in the "lower order" of thinking skills in Bloom's taxonomy), the identification of the "relevant" facts in a legal problem is not a simple task. What's relevant and what's not is at the heart of many legal disputes and disagreements over what is relevant and what is not dictate which precedents (i.e., prior court decisions in "similar" cases) will be applied to the resolution of the dispute. The same "facts" often lead to differing results depending on the weight each fact is given in the overall controversy (for example, in a simple negligence lawsuit, the jury must allocate each party's, including the plaintiff's, degree of fault in causing the injury). The "fact" phase of the analysis requires students to ask good questions to explore all aspects of the issue. For example, questions to fill in the missing information, and gauge the importance of each fact; questions to frame the current controversy with precedents from other cases, and question to explore how *changing the facts* would affect the result in the case.

The *Issue* is the *question* (or questions) that needs to be resolved. The identification of the issue is the most important step in the legal reasoning process and dictates every other step in reaching the conclusion. Students often have difficulty figuring out what the parties are arguing about. What is the controversy? What needs to be resolved? The answers to those questions often circle back to seeking out and reordering the relevant facts (for example, what kind of shoes was the plaintiff wearing when she slipped?). In addition, creative ways of looking at the situation may lead to additional, less obvious legal issues (for example, a breach of contract dispute may involve an unconscionability defense).

Once the issue is identified (of course, there may be many issues) the *Rule* needs to be determined. What precedents apply? What laws or regulations? What are the criteria by which this issue is resolved. Notice that misidentification of the issue will lead to the wrong rule and never lend itself to resolving the problem (so for example, you could read every treatise on contract law but if the problem is a tort problem it serves no purpose). Again the *question* governs and guides the entire legal reasoning process.

I call the *FIR* of *FIRAC* the "building blocks" of the problem. By working through these first three aspects of a legal issue (and reworking them), students organize their thinking about the problem. I like my students to do this in an outline form which makes it easier for them to also get an overview of the situation and each of the parts. And by organizing their thoughts *before* they start writing, they can write thought-out and well-organized essay for their analysis and conclusion. The outline format also lends itself to peer-to-peer review, with students evaluating and improving each others' outlines.

Once the *FIR* outline is developed, students analyze the problem by applying the Rule to the Facts (or alternatively, develop arguments for one or both sides) to reach a Conclusion (the *ac*). A good analysis (or argument) needs to incorporate and integrate each of the first three elements to justify the Conclusion. I find it best to have students do this portion of the problem in writing, which has the additional benefit of helping them develop skills in writing essays.

I asked my Business Law students at the end of the semester what benefits, if any, they felt they derived from the *FIRAC* methodology. One student responded: "I'm going to start by saying that "*FIRAC*" has vastly improved my critical thinking skills…"*FIRAC*" is without a doubt a valuable way to break these cases down to give you a much clearer perspective of the solutions to these problems." This student failed the first exam (all essay), showing great improvement by receiving a B—on the final (with 35 out of 40 points for the essays).

Another student wrote: "Using "*FIRAC*" this semester has been a helpful agent not only for Business Law but the courses in thinking critical. *FIRAC* is a simple way but best way to provide a good argument for any type of essay whether it's English, science, or even a business letter. *FIRAC* has helped me along lines to get a essay started by breaking down exactly I need as far facts and issue were concern with but overall the process help me out in many areas of writing in college". This student, who clearly has some academic deficiencies in his writing skills, improved from a D to a C in the final exam (with 30 out of 40 points for the essay portion).

My best student (straight A throughout the semester) also found the methodology highly beneficial. This student wrote: "I used *FIRAC* in almost, if not every problem and test. It gave me a system for answering the cases. *FIRAC* set up an organized way of breaking down the problems and coming to a conclusion. It made it much easier, for me, to come up with an approach and to focus on where I can go to figure out the answer, and not miss anything important in the problem. *FIRAC* has improved my critical thinking. Before, I don't think I was as good at taking a lot of information and breaking it down into something that I could work with".

Although extremely helpful to those students who practice the methodology, out of a class of 16 students (virtually all of whom found it useful to some degree), only 7 (less than half) scored higher on the final exam than the first exam in the course. Although certainly attributable to many other factors, I do believe that those students who did improve (and perhaps some who didn't), did improve their question asking skills by practicing *FIRAC* throughout the semester.

Although I primarily use *FIRAC* in my Business Law classes, this methodology can be adapted to any problem-solving context. And similarly to solving a legal problem, figuring out "What is the Question"? is an essential step in the critical/creative thinking process. Some of the questions students need to ask when using *FIRAC* are attached.

Forceful and Powerful Questions

In his book, *Learning to Think Things Through: A Guide to Critical Thinking Across the Curriculum* (Prentice Hall, 2001), Gerald M. Nosich explains how critical thinking begins with asking questions. Distinguishing critical thinking from problem solving, in which the problem is presented to a student, he notes that *critical thinking* on the other hand is "*noticing* that there are questions that need to be addressed" (p. 7). Applying that premise to the process of thinking critically in a discipline then requires students to identify and work through the central questions in the course. Learning for example to think like a manager, and learning to use the core and pervasive concepts ("forceful and powerful" concepts in Nosich's language) to address managerial questions, rather than merely learning *about* management. These central questions and concepts form the architecture of the discipline, integrate the various component parts, and provide the foundation for the students to develop their own questions. Notice how this approach requires active, rather than passive, learning on the students' part (as well as utilizing their creative abilities).

Students need help with identifying and working through the central questions in their courses. Without those integrating themes, the course material remains an assemblage of unrelated information without any logic or application. And without the architecture of these central questions, students' aren't oriented to develop good questions to make the material their "own".

One example of how I've used this concept (although I began long before ever reading Nosich) is to provide my Business Law students with critical thinking questions which help students identify and think about the central questions and core concepts in the topic. Business Law lends itself extremely well to this approach since many of the same questions and concepts appear throughout the discipline.

For example, a number of critical thinking questions I use in my Business Law class asks students to think about the standards that are used to evaluate legal liability and the role of the "reasonable person" standard in providing an objective, rather than a subjective standard. Once introduced at the beginning of the semester, these questions serve as integrating themes throughout the semester, and encourage the students to ask more specific, related questions to each new topic. For example, in torts, we might discuss whether a "reasonable person" would have acted in a certain way in connection with a negligent or intentional tort; in contracts we might discuss whether a "reasonable person" would have willing entered into that contract; in strict product liability, we might discuss whether a "reasonable person" would have appreciated the risks of using a product lacking a specific warning. And of course, what the heck is a "reasonable person" anyway!

Not only do students learn to appreciate the logic of a discipline by identifying and working through central questions, they also learn the importance of *ASKING QUESTIONS* to understand that discipline. Attached are some of the critical thinking questions I use in the torts section of my Business Law class.

Conclusion

Encouraging and helping students to develop good questioning skills, and to make asking questions habitual, is one of the most effective ways I know to spark our students' critical thinking and creative potential, and turn passive into active learners. In every course we teach, regardless of the discipline, students should get the message: "The Question is the Answer".

Question Rubric

	Good	Poor
Relevance to Issues	Comprehensive coverage of important issues	Focuses on unimportant issues/misses important issues
Information	Seeks important/unknown information	Seeks unimportant, obvious, and/or known facts
Purpose	Answers will enhance understanding of issue	Answers will contribute little to understanding of issue
Personally Meaningful	Question relates to personal experiences; answers will contribute to self—knowledge	Question seeks personally meaningless information
Expression	Question is clear and focused	Question is vague; point of question is ambiguous
Format	Bloom's category is properly labeled; multiple question types are utilized	Bloom's category is improperly labeled; question types are limited
English Usage	Correct use of grammar and usage (e.g., tenses, spelling, punctuation, sentence structure)	Grammar and usage mistakes

Questions for *FIRAC* Method of Analysis

Facts:

What are the relevant facts in the case or problem?
(Eliminate irrelevant facts).

Which facts are most important in this context? Prioritize.

Are there any significant facts missing?

What factual evidence has been introduced? What assumptions or value judgments?

What facts can be/are being used in your/Court's argument?
In reaching the conclusion?

How would changing one/some of the facts affect the outcome?

Issue:

What is the question(s) that needs to be answered?
(The issue should be in the form of a question).

What are the parties arguing about? (Eliminate points not in dispute).

What is the Court being asked to decide?

Rule:

What criteria have been used to decide this type of issue in the past?

Is there a relevant precedent (i.e., court opinion)?

Is there a relevant statute, regulation, or public policy?

Does the text offer any guidelines that have been used to resolve this type of problem?

Are there any conflicts between rules (e.g. between different precedents)?

If there is a conflict, which rule should apply to problem?

What are the similarities/differences between present problem and precedents being applied?

Are there any reasons why precedents should not apply here (e.g., distinguishable facts, change in values, public policy considerations)?

What are the reasons offered by the Court to support its conclusion?

Application: (Analysis, Argument):

Applying the relevant rules to the facts of this problem, what is your/the Court's resolution of the issue?

What weaknesses do you see in the other side's arguments?

Why did the Court reach the conclusion it did?

Is the Court attempting to balance competing interests?

Are there any flaws in the Court's analysis? Are arguments just rationalizations to support desired outcome?

Is your/the Court's resolution fair? Is there a compromise solution which will meet the legitimate needs of both sides?

Indicator words: look for words like: because; as a result of, due to, in view of, by reason of, on account of.

Conclusion:

Briefly, how have you decided the issue and why?

What's the answer to the question?

Indicator words: look for words like: therefore, thus, as a result of, it follows that.

Business Law I Critical Thinking Questions
Chapters 5–9

Chapter 5.

1. What is the meaning of "intent" in tort law? Does a tortuous act require a harmful motive?

2. What role does the "reasonable person" standard play in the intentional torts? In the tort of negligence?

3. Tort law provides remedies for injuries to only certain personal and property interests. How are these "protected interests" determined? Can you think of an interest that isn't protected?

4. What role does "foreseeability" play in the tort of negligence? What role does foreseeability play in proximate cause? In the duty of care? (See the Palsgraf case).

5. Bona fide competitive behavior is a recognized defense to the torts based on unfair competition. What determines whether competitive behavior is "bona fide" or tortuous?

Chapter 6

1. Do you think it is fair to hold a retailer "strictly liable" for damages resulting from a product sold by the retailer even when he/she exercised all possible care in the preparation and sale of the product?

2. What are the reasons for imposing strict liability as a matter of public policy? Do you agree or disagree with these reasons?

3. What is an "unreasonably" dangerous product?

4. Are there "reasonably dangerous" products?

5. How does the concept of the "reasonable person" relate to an "unreasonably dangerous/reasonably dangerous" product?

6. What role does "foreseeability" play in the tort of strict liability?

7.   What role does "proximate cause" play in the tort of strict liability?

Chapter 7

1.   Notice that unlike the duration of property rights in tangible property, the duration for property rights in intellectual property are limited in time. Why so you think this is so?

References

Bloom, B.S. (Ed.) (1956) Taxonomy of educational objectives: The classification of educational goals: Handbook I, cognitive domain. New York ; Toronto: Longmans, Green.

Chaffee, John, McMahon Christine, Stout, Barbara: *Critical Thinking, Thoughtful Writings, A Rhetoric with Readings.* 3rd Ed. Boston: Houghton Mifflin Company, 2005.

Nosich, Gerald M: *Learning to Think Things Through, A Guide to Critical Thinking Across the Curriculum.* New Jersey: Prentice Hall, 2001.

Lessons Learned: Engaging Students by Creating Community in Online Courses

James W. Brown, Ph.D.

A key to successful online courses is creating a sense of community in the online classroom. Learning communities have restructured the classroom and form a collaborative pedagogy that has dramatically increased student involvement, learning and persistence. Students spend more time with their peers and more time on class matters in a cooperative and collaborative manner. Students are engaged both inside and outside the classroom, which serves to involve the students more fully in the academic matters. The students see their peers and faculty as more supportive of their needs. As a result of all of this, they spend more time studying and are more engaged in the learning process. It fosters almost a military "foxhole" frame of mind where a "we can get though this if we all stick together" attitude prevails. Creating these types of highly successful learning communities within the online classroom has been a challenge.

The Concept of Building Community in the Online Classroom

Human beings have a basic need to communicate in groups. Throughout history human beings organized themselves in groups or networks such as tribes, clans, villages or even the basic family unit. Webster's Dictionary defines a community as "any group living in the same area or having interests, work, etc. in common." Today the limitation of geography has changed because of the digital universe and the entire concept of community must be redefined. Shaffer and Anundsen (1993) define community as a dynamic whole that emerges when people share common practices, are interdependent, make decisions jointly, and identify themselves with something larger than the sum of their individual relationships. One of the most powerful effects of using the Internet for teaching and learning has been its ability to produce virtual communities that link people together and form cohesive groups. The Latin root, found in the word "community" and "communicate," means to share. As students share life experiences related to the course content, other students have the opportunity to benefit from perspectives that may not be available through the instructor. Learning becomes multidirectional and the community develops into a boundary-less container of knowledge and experience.

Palloff and Pratt (1999) identify developing a sense of community within the group of online learners as the key ingredient for making the learning process successful. The online community develops a sense of interaction, a sense of feeling connected, a sense of engagement and a sense of belonging. The dynamics of creating community online are similar to that of group dynamics where the group goes through Tuckman's stages of forming, norming, storming, performing, and adjourning (Tuckman, p. 384-399). The student must "feel" the sense of connectedness when they enter the course. Specific places need to be designed for students to gather and discuss what is happening in the course today. If the student enters the course and sees that there has been no activity in the past several days they feel abandoned and discouraged. It is as though they have arrived in the classroom and found no one there. This can rapidly destroy the sense of community. An important instructor responsibility is to constantly check the course and gently guide the conversation by infusing a challenging question for discussion or offering a well timed note of praise for a particularly insightful response.

The benefit of creating community in the online classroom is that it produces better learning, better retention and greater satisfaction. Hill, Raven and Han (p. 383-393) admit that historically drop out rates in distance education courses have been significant, ranging from 30 to 50 percent. In their study of online courses designed to build community, the retention rate was raised to 94 percent with a high degree of satisfaction.

Karen Swan (p. 23-27) collected data from 22 courses online courses and studied the course design factors that were associated with course success. Her findings demonstrated that three factors were associated with the success of online courses: (1) interaction with course content, (2) interaction with course instructors, and (3) interaction among course participants. The development of learning communities is critical to the success of online courses.

Building community in the classroom has always been part of education. Current research shows that for the online instructor, building community is an essential part of the successful online course and not a supplementary nicety of the course. Community does not just happen in an online environment, it was be carefully planned for, nurtured, energized, and built in as an integral part of the course.

My Experiences with Online Course Development

I developed the first online course in the College of Professional Studies at New Jersey City University and became the "college expert" who helped other professors do the same. As an Assistant Dean, a significant portion of my job was to formally help other faculty members develop their online courses. We progressed to the point where we hired a full-time instructional designer and support staff and my role shifted to that of quality assurance. I helped professors get started and then reviewed their finished courses before they went live. At the same time, I continued to teach and develop my own online and web assisted courses which became my laboratory for trying out new techniques and different features. Some of these worked well and some did not. I am now the Dean of Health Sciences and Human Performance at Ocean County College where we are placing a substantial portion of the Associate Degree Nursing Program in a web-assisted format where students will receive all of their clinical, nursing laboratory and face-to-face instruction one day per week and the rest of their content will be delivered online. The following are practical strategies and examples that I found personally successful in developing and delivering successful online courses.

Breaking the Ice in an Online Environment: Share something personal

Several online and web-assisted courses were created to foster the sense of community among the online students. Specific features of the course design allowed students to interact socially as well as academically. Typical of all online courses, students begin the class nervous and unsure about their ability to connect to the class site. An immediate ice-breaker is the use of a small but highly effective introduction and photo area. The first assignment asks students to share with the class about themselves and to provide a photo if possible. If the students are not able to provide a digital photo or scan one in, the instructor scans it in for them. The student finds a picture of the instructor with their family or pet and a paragraph about their interests, family, hobbies, pets, etc. when they begin the course.

The instructor models for the student how their introduction should appear. By using this as the first assignment, it gives the student a "fun" way to begin the course and starts to build the learning community. I typically share a picture of my family and give them a little detail of what is happening right now in my life.

I have shared our wedding photos and our family's cruise to the Caribbean. It helped to set the tone for the entire course, and presented the instructor as someone who is friendly, approachable, and willing to share.

The students typically responded enthusiastically to this and would post similar information about their lives. The "cat person" would post a number of pictures of them interacting with their cat. Similarly a "dog person" would comment about the special wonder and attributes associated with their pet. It immediately sets up the sense of community similar to that which forms around the watercooler or in the break-room in the workplace. Although many students are initially reluctant to share a picture of themselves, within the first few weeks of the course most students have shared a personal introduction and have included a picture.

After the "ice is broken," students feel more comfortable discussing things of a personal nature or a personal experience related to the course topic. Swan (p. 23-27) refers to this as self-disclosure which is defined as the sharing of personal information, usually of a vulnerable nature. Self-disclosure is an immediacy behavior that is frequently employed by instructors to lesson the gap between themselves and their students. The students also used self-disclosure which in Swan's study evoked the greatest number and depth of responses from the other students.

Have students create their own Homepage

Some course delivery platforms such as Blackboard, WebCT and eCollege provide the student with the ability to produce their own web page. In WebCT for example, the student homepage tool is a basic web page editor designed to allow students to share a message about themselves with the rest of the class. This personal online message is stored in a Student Homepage. Instructors may use this tool as a method of personalizing an online course. The Student Homepage content options may include: a short description about the student, an image of the student and links to other web sites. Students would click on the WebCT Student Homepage Tool to see a screen that lists other students in the class that had created their own student homepages and be able to add their own. My experience has been that only a few of the more "techy" students will attempt this and the other students who are not able to do this feel threatened by the technology.

Design a warm and friendly online classroom

The look and feel of the online course is important. There should be an instant "curb appeal" when the student enters the course.

Dr. Lilliam Rosado the Department Chair in Health Sciences at NJCU used a series of pictures drawn by her young daughter Mia to illustrate her entire course. She was teaching online courses primarily to school nurses and used a series of classroom images of the teacher, the student, the blackboard, the teachers desk, an the apple for the teacher. She cleverly used the apple drawn by her daughter as her "bullets" to illustrate important points. It was highly effective. The fact that much of the colorful graphics were drawn by her daughter eliminated copyright issues and provided a very personal image of the instructor throughout the entire course.

Make Attendance and Participation Mandatory

In order for students to participate and be part of the community in the online course they need to **be** there. I have always required class participation and made it worth at least 10% of the grade. The formal policy was stated clearly in the online syllabus. Students who were not participating early in the course would receive gentle reminders sent as personal e-mails. I would also send out reminders to the entire class letting them know it is not how many times they participate but it is the quality of that participation.

I believe a key to the success of my online courses was that I would carefully observe if a student had not signed into the course. If they had not signed on within 72 hours after the course started, I would call them to see if they were having a problem. I would try to address their problem immediately and reassure them that ultimately, they would be successful. Fear of using technology and a lack of confidence is common place at the very beginning of the course. Within a few hours, a student can feel so frustrated that they want to give up. The instructor can act as a catalyst to help the student climb an initial steep learning curve. If the instructor provides an "intensive care" during the first two weeks of the course the students quickly gain confidence and learn that almost everyone else feels the same way. I consistently experience 95% retention rates through this investment of time right at the beginning of the course.

Go after the "Lurkers" and Engage Them

There are students who will read the online discussions and postings by other students but will not participate in the discussion. These individuals have been referred to as "Lurkers." Many students have different learning styles and the lurkers may be the equivalent of "good listeners" in the face-to-face classroom and have a valid and highly effective learning style. They need to be treated gently by the instructor and be encouraged to participate. Many instructors assign a point value for attendance and participation. It is important to make it clear to the students exactly how they can earn these participation points.

New Jersey City University, located in Jersey City, New Jersey, is currently in one of the major gateways to the United States. Immigrants to the United States coming to the Port of New York through the three major airports, settle down in many communities in Northern New Jersey. This region is probably one of the most culturally diverse communities in the country. NJCU's student population is comprised of students from over 65 countries speaking over 30 different languages on campus. Many students come to campus with poor written communication skills in English, since English is often their second language. This presents particular problems for the online instructor and lurking becomes a major challenge. Notwithstanding, participation in online courses forces students to write and thereby improve their written communication skills. The major course management systems such as WebCT, eCollege and BlackBoard make it easy for the online instructor to detect lurking. The instructor can easily determine what pages have been visited, how long they have been visited, and how many times the student has contributed compared to other students.

I try to give students helpful hints to improve their online communication. I have created a section where they are shown, step-by-step, with helpful screen shots how to check their spelling and grammar using Microsoft Word and then paste their responses into a discussion post. I insist that spelling and grammar count no matter what subject is being taught. This really helps to reinforce the cross-curricular competency of written communication. Students with limited English proficiency quickly find that online courses provide the time and tools necessary for them to organize their thoughts and revise their responses over and over again before they post them. The final product is much better than posting a first draft. They prefer the time delay that asynchronous learning provides. As an instructor, you may notice that their asynchronous posts in the discussion area are of a higher quality that the ones in the synchronous chat area.

After the students are using the tools such as a spell checker and a grammar checker and have learned how to copy and paste, a whole new on line world is created for them. One Latino student commented as follows:

> *"Dr. Brown, I was always conscious about speaking up in class because of my thick accent. The trick you taught us of writing in Microsoft Word and checking our spelling and grammar before posting has helped me tremendously. I am no longer afraid to share my opinion because I have time to think and change what I want to*

*say before anyone sees it. I find I am doing the same thing at work if I have to send
an e-mail to someone. Thanks."*

Many students that have English as a first language also prefer having additional time to think and reflect before they have to post, producing a much higher-order mental process which involves logic, imagination, and deep thought. Instructors who teach both face-to-face and online have noticed that there may be more critical thinking in the asynchronous online environment than in their face-to-face classroom.

There is an art to encouraging students to become engaged online and join in the discussions. Lurkers must be gently prodded to take that bold step and join the discussion. If the lurkers are not drawn out the more outgoing Myers Briggs "E" types will dominate the discussions. However, care must be taken in the approach since being perceived as overly aggressive will discourage rather than encourage some lurkers, resulting in course withdrawal.

Instructors role as Playground Monitor: Courtesy, Honesty and Respect

Setting a tone of mutual respect and courtesy in the course is important to establish the feeling of safety within the community. The course should provide a safe environment for the students to share ideas without the fear of being harshly criticized or chastised. I always put the following statement into the course to try to set a tone of respect:

> *"The tone of this assessment should be helpful and respectful and not critical. Conduct yourself as if you are giving advice to a trusted friend. You may actually make one in the process!"*

The student should feel as safe as they do in their homes or with their friends. This is a critical role for the instructor to constantly monitor the discussion and step in when it needs to be corrected. A harsh word or inappropriate statement can quickly shut down communication and destroy the sense of community. In many respects the instructor acts as a "playground monitor" allowing each student to interact cooperatively with the other to build creations out of the sand. They need to create an atmosphere of inclusion and safety where participants need to be able to speak and debate their ideas without fear of retribution or destructive criticism.

Course management systems allow the instructor to "whisper" to a student so they can communicate without others seeing what you are writing. You can also privately e-mail a student about an unkind word or a sarcastic remark. I have actually called a student up on the phone to discuss their behavior online. Conversely, praising students for an especially insightful or thought provoking statement can inspire students to come out of their shells and provide a rich environment where ideas, philosophies, personal experiences can be shared with the group. The rules of Netiquette or online good online "manners" should be clearly established at the beginning of the course. I place the rules of netiquette upfront in the online syllabus where I outline and emphasize what is expected of online behavior. I also reinforce this in the assignment and discussion areas of the course.

Use of Small Groups within the Course

The use of the threaded discussion area has become the predominant tool used by most educational institutions around the world to support the online learning process. The goal was to move beyond this to include other tools and strategies which would foster an even greater cense of community and culture of learning online. Combining students into small groups to work on a particular project promotes collaborative and cooperative learning. Most students, particularly the online students, would prefer to work alone and not have to rely on others to complete a project. Working in small groups on a collaborative basis is an essential function of almost any work environment. Sharing files electronically, downloading and uploading information has become a routine skill that must be mastered to survive in today's job market.

The group project compels students to e-mail each other, to use the chat rooms strategically at pre-arrainged times, or even set up conference calls between themselves. The use of a reflective letter along with the project provides the instructor with insight into exactly what each student in the group is doing and their contribution to the group process. This reduces the incidence of students who do not contribute or provide minimal contribution to group work, and slide by because others in the group "pick up the slack." The reflective letter describing their experience within the group and contribution to the group helps to expose the "slackers" and draw them into the process.

The Use of Peer-Coaching to Build Community

Another opportunity to build community is the use of peer coaching for term papers or research papers. One recurrent problem, especially with the urban student, was the ability to write. Traditionally, the instructor would help the student narrow the topic to something manageable, the student would then submit the completed paper at the end of the course and the instructor would attach comments to the paper and assign a grade (evaluation). The quality of the research papers dramatically increased by introducing peer coaching or peer assessment to the writing process.

1. The student begins by submitting the first draft to another student (the peer coach) and not to the instructor.

2. The peer coach is provided with a rubric on how to assess a paper and returns the first draft with their comments to the author.

3. The author then rewrites the paper based upon the peer feedback.

4. The second draft is then submitted with the peer assessment to the online instructor.

5. The instructor attaches their suggestions and comments and then returns it to the student without a grade.

6. The student then produces the final draft which is submitted for a grade. The peer coach also receives a grade for the quality of their peer assessment.

The student learns the value of refining their written work through the process of peer assessment and revision. Students use rubrics as a guide to develop, revise and judge their own work. A key ingredient in learner-centered teaching is providing students with the feedback necessary to enable them to improve their work. By using peer coaches they receive this valuable feedback not only from their instructor but from their peers as well. This further strengthens the community in the course.

The Online Field Trip

It is good to host activities that are synchronous as well as asynchronous. The online field trip is an excellent synchronous tool that can add a high level of excitement to the online course. I can remember as a child in grammar school looking forward to a scheduled field trip to a dairy farm or the Franklin Institute in Philadelphia. I would think about it for weeks. The online field trip can do the same thing in the online or web-assisted course. This tool works well to build community and generate a real sense of excitement in a course.

One of my mountaintop experiences in teaching was providing the opportunity for the entire graduate Managed Healthcare class to meet online with Congressman Menendez right in the heat of intense debates on Capitol Hill when the Patient's Bill of Rights was nearing a House vote. The students practiced in the live chat rooms days before they went live with the Congressman's staff. The Congressman was in his Washington Office with his key staffer on healthcare when he went online with our students who participated from various locations throughout Northern New Jersey, as well as Mississippi, Alabama and Rhode Island. The Congressman shared the intimate details of the back room horse trading that was necessary to move the Bill forward. It was a fun and team-building experience and one they could not have experienced anywhere but online. Class enthusiasm continued for weeks, and it led to a period of rich discussion in the class that was a joy to be a part of.

Since that time other guest speakers such as corporate managed care executives and State Epidemiologists have been invited into the course. We have also organized several different face-to-face field trips which have been trips to Washington DC and Trenton NJ to meet key people in government and industry. A student writes:

> *"Dr. Brown, The experience I had of getting online with Congressman Menendez was the most fantastic experience I have ever had in school. It went beyond what you could ever read in a text book. We really learned what is going on at this second in Congress and that there is so much more there than you would ever hear or read about. It really has inspired me to becoming more involved with government. It was unbelievable."*

Conclusions: Sponges versus Coral

Rena Palloff (public presentation, August 2002) uses the analogy of the sponge versus the coral with respect to building community in online courses. The sponge just sits their and soaks up the nutrients and water and doesn't substantially contribute to the ecosystem around it. They show so little movement that until the 18th century naturalists considered them plants. Many students in an online course will just sit there as a sponge, taking in the wealth of the course but contributing little. Whereas the coral, which makes up coral reef, is the building platform for a whole thriving, living ecosystem. "Corals build community by each secreting their resources to build the reef and mutually support the group." The Coral protects and strengthens the entire ecosystem. The coral reefs are found in gentle warm seas that support the delicate biological community. The coral will add new layers to that which was built before. The coral is analogous to the optimum online community where students and instructor support and protect one another and all secrete rich nutrients to allow the growth of knowledge and support the delicate process of learning.

What are the outcomes of building community in the online course environment? The use of the above techniques have resulted in excellent retention rates of 95% or greater, considerably higher than the 70-75% national average for online courses. The course evaluations are also exceptional, citing the value of the online learning community to the success of the online learning experience. The experiences of both instructor and students have been to enjoy one of the richest educational and learning environments.

References

Hill, J., Raven, A., & Han S. (2002). Connections in web-based learning environments: a research-based model for community building. *Quarterly Review of Distance Education*, 3(4), 383-393.

Palloff, R., & Pratt, K. (1999). *Building learning communities in cyberspace: effective strategies for the online classroom.* 1st ed. San Francisco: Jossey-Bass, Inc.

Shaffer, C., & Anundsen, K. (1993). *Creating community anywhere: finding support and connection in a fragmented world.* New York: Tarcher/Perigree.

Swan, K. (2002). Building learning communities in online courses: the importance of interaction. *Education, Communication and Information*, 2(1), 23-27.

Tuckman, B. W (1965). Developmental sequence in small groups. *Psychological Bulletin*, 63, 384-399.

About the Consultants/Editors

Dr. Sharon L. Silverman

Dr. Sharon L. Silverman is currently in private practice as an educational consultant. Highlights of her work in higher education include faculty development in teaching and learning, student retention initiatives, and international learning experiences. She is the co-founder of a non-profit organization, *Crossing the Border*, focusing on international projects that promote peace and learning across cultures. Her experiences as a Fulbright Senior Scholar (1999) and as a Rotary Foundation Scholar (2002) in South Africa led her to develop a project called *Sharing Cultures* that connects college students in the USA with those in South Africa in a virtual learning environment. Her publications include two books co-authored with Martha Casazza and the lead article in this book reprinted from the *Learning Assistance Review*. A lifetime resident of Chicago, Dr. Silverman loves adventure and travel and had one of her greatest adventures riding a motorcycle in Australia and camping in the Outback.

Dr. Martha E. Casazza

Dr. Martha E. Casazza is the Dean of the College of Arts and Sciences at National-Louis University in Chicago, Illinois. She is a regular contributor to professional journals in the field of education and is currently researching an oral history of access to higher education in the United States which she hopes to publish soon. She was one of the first to call for a theoretical foundation for the field of developmental education in her *Journal of Developmental Education* article, "Strengthening Practice with Theory. Dr. Casazza was a Senior Fulbright Scholar in South Africa in 1999 where she was able to combine her professional interests with her love for travel and building cross cultural relationships. In addition to traveling, Dr.Casazza enjoys biking along the lakefront in Chicago.

978-0-595-35067-4
0-595-35067-4